JOHNNY CIAO'S KONCERT KITCHEN

Johnny Ciao's Koncert Kitchen

100 Recipes from America's "Culinary Rocker"

JOHNNY CIAO

HPBooks

HPBooks
Published by The Berkley Publishing Group
200 Madison Avenue
New York, NY 10016

Copyright © 1996 by John Persico
Book design by Richard Oriolo
Cover design by Joe Lanni
Cover illustration by Ed Wexler

First edition: December 1996

Published simultaneously in Canada.

The Putnam Berkley World Wide Web site address is
http://www.berkley.com/berkley

Library of Congress Cataloging-in-Publication Data

Ciao, Johnny.
    Johnny Ciao's koncert kitchen : 100 recipes from America's
"culinary rocker" / Johnny Ciao. — 1st ed.
        p.   cm.
    ISBN 1-55788-255-X
    1. Quick and easy cookery. I. Title.
TX833.5.C49 1996
641.5'55—dc20   96-13203
                                                           CIP

Printed in the United States of America

10 9 8 7 6 5 4 3 2 1

*T*his book is dedicated to my mom
and dad for their unrelenting support,
patience, guidance and love

CONTENTS

Introduction   ix

Rhythm Snax and Trax   1

Symphonic Soups and Salads   17

Pasta Percussions   33

Rockin' Poultry   47

Soulful Seafood   59

Meaty Orchestrations   79

Veggie Vocals   95

Drummin' Dips, Marinades and Dressings   107

Final Notes   121

Glossary   131

Johnny Ciao's Seasonings   135

Index   137

INTRODUCTION

*I*f you ask me what I love most, besides family and friends, I'll confess immediately that it's food and music. As the son of a ballroom dancer and a mother who never stops cooking, I've always lived with the combination of entertainment and eating. I grew up in an exuberant, extended Italian family who lived together—aunts, uncles, cousins, grandparents, open doors, the smell of food always in the air, music everywhere and lots of loud voices—in a six-family apartment building in New York City.

At a time when so many of my friends had no structured home life, it seemed like I was the only one who had to make up excuses for *not* hanging out, especially when it was time to eat. Three or more square meals a day, yes indeed. God forbid I didn't show. In retrospect, I'm glad it went that way. It's the kind of family experience that seems to be quickly disappearing.

The '70s and '80s brought about an eating revolution of sorts. Fast-food chains and microwaves proliferated. Families weren't gathering around the dining room table like they used to. Mom was now going to work to help support the family. Time to spend in the kitchen was now at a premium.

When I left home to live on my own in the early '70s, I was faced with a major dilemma. With little money and not a lot of time to spend in the kitchen, how could I keep on eating the way I'd enjoyed at home? Although I've had some formal culinary training over the years, most of my kitchen knowledge comes from the first-hand experience and exposure I got from the time I could walk. And it was during those lean years of cooking for myself that I came to create the best foods for less. From healthy soups that cost pennies to improv meatloafs and new slants on traditional European dishes, I always managed to treat friends, houseguests and myself to terrific meals.

My culinary and entertainment careers first crossed in the mid-'70s while I was working as the first white disc jockey on an urban radio station in St. Petersburg, Florida. For personal appearances, I performed under the stage name of Johnny Snow at large cookouts and remotes around St. Pete's. I then went on to promote rock concerts at large Tampa Bay facilities, including the Sunshine Speedway, where I not only promoted rock shows, but voluntarily worked the backstage grill. It was always a thrill to watch these rock stars enjoy the "sounds" of my cooking. After a few years in Florida, I decided to move to Atlanta, Georgia, to promote mainstream musicians and popular jazz artists, including Ramsey Lewis, Stanley Turrentine, Jimmy Smith, Eric Gale, Woody Shaw and others. I ran these jazz concerts from an office in the City Hall Annex Building, where I met many Atlanta dignitaries and celebrities, many of whom were invited into my kitchen.

Several years later I began a communications firm and worked with such clients as home-run king Henry (Hank) Aaron, Isaac Hayes, long-distance runner Stan Cottrell, Georgia Tech running coach Mike Spino and a host of local musicians, politicians and businesses. Hank Aaron always requested that I cook Italian food for him and his family and friends. In the mid-'80s, I opened a Beverly Hills office to provide marketing services to the home-video industry, and worked with such artists as Michael Nesmith, Hank Williams, Jr., Divine, Pia Zadora and Jermaine Jackson. And in 1984 I had the opportunity to bring together the two things I love most, food and music, when I produced a book and video package called *Cooking with Country Stars*. It featured recipes, bios and photographs of more than forty country-music performers, including Dolly Parton, Charlie Daniels, the Oak Ridge Boys, Barbara Mandrell, Minnie Pearl and Hank Williams. The book went on to sell over a half million copies.

While producing the television show *FM Magazine*, I took a film crew backstage at the annual Willie Nelson Picnic. Even though there was lots of good old southern food everywhere, someone in my crew who knew my passion for cooking suggested I whip up something special for the guests. With raw materials scavenged from the supplies on hand, within minutes Willie, Waylon Jennings, Merle Haggard, Linda Ronstadt and others were munching down on my Texas Prawn Stew. This really signaled the unofficial start of my cooking career, and I was to abandon my producer's role for a chef's apron.

My first professional culinary gig as Johnny Ciao, the "Culinary Rocker," was at the Bay Area Music Awards (Bammies), where I fixed food for a thousand, including such music greats as Carlos Santana, Huey Lewis, Sammy Hagar, the Grateful Dead, Jefferson Starship and Chris Isaac. I guess you could say I plunged into the deep end of the cooking business.

Then, with more chutzpah than professional experience, I approached a Beverly Hills chef's agent for a gig in a private home—my ambition was to be groovin' in the kitchen of some superstar or Hollywood mogul. The agent set me up with a couple of interviews, but these people, in their pseudo-Tudor mansions and sprawling haciendas, were looking for a "central-casting" chef—someone who'd cooked for minor royalty. I didn't fit the bill. When my agent suggested an interview with Michael Jackson, I jumped at the chance to meet the legendary "Gloved One," no matter what the outcome.

I wasn't "auditioned" personally by Michael, but I knew he was in the next room, within ear- and eyeshot. I guess there was something about me that clicked because I got the call-back within two hours—the job was mine.

Officially I was hired as Michael's personal chef, but before long I was taking on the role of an informal, new-wave major domo—organizing the pantries, the household staff and whatever job needed to be done, including "fattening up" my new boss.

Michael had just come off the *Bad* tour. He was extremely thin and run-down. I had to figure out his food preferences and his typically eccentric eating habits. Because he loved to eat with his hands, many of the dishes were created as finger food. I also cut his intake of dairy products, including massive amounts of cheese. Michael didn't react well to heavy, red meat dishes. Even fish and poultry were called "flesh" in the Jackson household, but I did manage to reintroduce both into his diet. Each day it was my responsibility to present him with a menu. It had to be as inventive as any restaurant fare, so I created names for each of the dishes (many of which appear in this book) and lively descriptions to make the bill of fare as appealing as possible.

Cooking for Michael Jackson was both interesting and challenging, but it was his many guests and celebrity friends, from Marlon Brando and Emmanuel Lewis to Gregory Peck and Whitney Houston, that made Neverland such a lively and demanding gig.

*   *   *

Great food doesn't have to be expensive or difficult to prepare. Whether it's for a fancy party or a family meal in the kitchen, cooking should be a fun experience. Personally, I'd go so far as to say that cooking can be a sort of religious experience—a meditational process whereby slicing, dicing and mixing are like the act of prayer. No matter how much or how little time I've got, I love to turn the preparation of food into a relaxing and energizing part of my day.

With a moniker like the "culinary rocker," you know I fill my kitchen with the sounds I like best—rock, jazz and blues. You'll even hear the occasional aria or big band sound accompanying the chopping and bashing. Getting my friends and family together—most likely crowded into the kitchen—to create a party out of the making of a great meal is the best way I know to turn a daily chore into an act of sharing. Even if I'm alone I cook up lots of extras to freeze or to use in the next day's dish.

Cooking for yourself, your friends and family shouldn't be a test of culinary skill and patience. It should be satisfying and relaxing. Throughout this book I've tried to give you inventive, healthy, homey and happy foods. I want to help you make the process of cooking and eating more joyful. That's what *Johnny Ciao's Koncert Kitchen* is all about—orchestrating the best times and food with the least hassle.

JOHNNY CIAO'S KONCERT KITCHEN

Rhythm Snax and Trax

GREAT BALLS OF FIRE

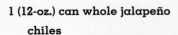

1 (12-oz.) can whole jalapeño
   chiles

1 1/2 cups (6 oz.) shredded
   sharp Cheddar cheese

1 cup buttermilk baking mix

1 pound regular or spicy bulk
   Italian sausage

1 teaspoon Johnny Ciao's
   Country Herbs (see page
   136 for substitutions)

1/2 cup plain fine bread
   crumbs

*L*ike it hot? Want to cause a stir? Feed these to your friends, and check out the results.

*P*reheat oven to 400F (205C). Drain chiles and cut off stems. Rinse chiles and remove seeds. Carefully stuff chiles with cheese, then set aside.

*T*horoughly blend baking mix with sausage and any left-over cheese in a medium bowl. Form a large ice cream scoop–size ball from sausage mixture, then place a chile in the center, wrapping mixture around chile. Repeat with remaining sausage mixture and chiles.

*M*ix herbs and bread crumbs in a shallow bowl. Coat each chile with crumb mixture. Arrange chiles in a large baking pan. Bake 15 minutes or until golden brown.

Steve Edwards and Tawny Little try some of Johnny's Corny Shrimp on the set of *AM Los Angeles*.

CORNY SHRIMP

4 ears corn with husks

2 tablespoons olive oil

3 cloves garlic, minced

1 fresh jalapeño chile, minced

1/2 large white onion, chopped

1/2 red or yellow bell pepper, chopped

1 teaspoon Johnny Ciao's Soulful Seafood (see page 136 for substitutions)

1 pound shelled and deveined large shrimp, cut into quarters

4 cilantro sprigs, finely chopped

Johnny's Guac and Roll (page 118)

*T*his has become one of my signature dishes, which I created for Michael Jackson. It's an unusual and sensuous finger food . . . just don't get carried away and eat the corn husks.

*P*eel back corn husks from fresh corn and cut off near bottom of cob. Cut off corn kernels with a large knife to measure 1 cup. Set corn and husks aside.

*H*eat olive oil in a medium skillet over medium heat. Add garlic, chile, onion and bell pepper; sauté 3 minutes or until onion is softened. Add seasoning and corn; stir to combine. Reduce heat to low. Cook 1 minute, then add shrimp and cilantro. Cover and cook 2 minutes.

*D*ivide corn husks into bunches of 2 or 3 leaves, depending on size. Tie tops with a thin strand of corn husk to form boat shapes. Spoon shrimp mixture onto husks. Top with a dab of guacamole.

Variations

Pour mixture into tortillas for burrito magic. Makes 6 to 8 large burritos. Shrimp mixture can be served over pasta. Makes 4 servings with pasta.

DILLED MUSSELS

2 pounds large black mussels

1 cup water

2 tablespoons virgin olive oil

1 egg yolk

1/2 teaspoon white wine
**   vinegar**

1/2 teaspoon fresh lemon juice

1 teaspoon dry mustard

1 teaspoon dried dill weed

*W*hen I was growing up, we'd feast on mussels and clams fairly regularly. In the '60s, when it was still safe to eat the shellfish from the Long Island Sound we would gather bushels of fresh shellfish. Most of the time the mussels were prepared with a tomato base sauce, or eaten raw. This recipe is ideal when you've got lots of people to feed. It can be served hot from the pot or cold.

*R*inse and scrub mussels and remove beards. Discard any mussels that do not close when tapped. Place mussels and water in a large pot over medium heat. Cover and steam until mussels open completely. Discard any mussels that do not open. Cool mussels and remove one side of shell, leaving meat in other half of shell. Place mussels on a large platter.

*B*eat together olive oil, egg yolk, vinegar, lemon juice, mustard and dill in a small bowl until thickened. Adjust seasoning to taste. Top each mussel with a spoonful of mixture. Serve immediately or cover and refrigerate up to 4 hours.

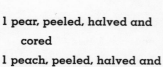 # FRUIT BOATS

1 pear, peeled, halved and
    cored
1 peach, peeled, halved and
    pitted
About 1/2 ripe banana
1/2 cup fresh raspberries or
    strawberries

2 tablespoons cranberry juice
2 heads Belgian endive,
    cleaned and separated
4 ounces Gorgonzola cheese,
    crumbled
2 tablespoons chopped
    walnuts

Combine all fruits and juice in a food processor or blender and process until pureed. Add more banana if mixture is too thin. Arrange endive on a large platter. Pour fruit mixture through a funnel into squeeze bottles, then squeeze onto each leaf. Sprinkle with cheese and walnuts.

Michael Jackson loved to eat with his hands so I created lots of finger foods. Salads are a bit of a challenge, but here's one that really works. It's great for parties, or for kids who will love the flavor, shape and taste.

HONEY-GLAZED CHICKEN STRIPS

*T*his sweet-tasting chicken dish is a favorite among kids, but with enough spice to please the most discriminating adult tastes.

1 pound skinless, boneless chicken breasts, sliced into thin strips
1/2 cup honey
1/3 cup Dijon mustard or other mustard
1 tablespoon low-sodium soy sauce
1 teaspoon chopped gingerroot
1/2 teaspoon Johnny Ciao's Country Herbs (see page 136 for substitutions)
2 cloves garlic, minced
2 tablespoons virgin olive oil
1 tablespoon fresh lemon juice

*P*reheat oven to 350F (175C) or preheat broiler. Arrange chicken in a large baking dish; set aside.

*M*ix together remaining ingredients in a medium bowl and pour over chicken, completely covering chicken with mixture. Let set about 15 minutes, turning chicken occasionally.

*B*ake 10 minutes or broil 3 to 4 minutes on each side until chicken is cooked through. Serve hot with wooden picks.

PEPPERMINT CHICKEN WINGS

12 large chicken wings

Salt

1 fresh jalapeño chile, seeded
   and minced

2 cloves garlic, minced

4 tablespoons finely chopped
   fresh mint leaves

1 (6-oz.) can tomato puree

2 tablespoons orange or lemon
   juice

1/2 cup water

Horseradish Marinade (page
   115) to serve (optional)

*R*inse chicken under cold running water and pat dry with paper towels. Sprinkle salt over the chicken and let stand 30 minutes.

*S*tir together chile, garlic, mint, tomato puree and citrus juice in a medium bowl. Add chicken to bowl and turn to coat chicken. Let marinate 15 to 30 minutes, turning several times.

*P*reheat oven to 400F (205C). Place wings and marinade in a baking dish. Pour water around, not over, chicken. Cover and bake 20 minutes. Remove lid and broil on each side 10 minutes. Enjoy while hot or cold. Serve with Horseradish Marinade, if desired.

*W*hile growing up, my family would hold huge gatherings year-round. Porterhouse steaks would be prepared with a special marinade that I wanted to use with nonbarbecued food. The secret ingredient in this marinade was mint. Here I've applied it to everyone's favorite, chicken wings.

RICE BALLS

*T*his old family fa-vorite is a treat. When Grandma or Mom made these, I'd flip, because they're oh so good. They are similar to Italian knishes. Try them and you'll see what I mean.

1 cup cooked white rice

2 tablespoons chopped
    prosciutto

1 egg

1 teaspoon Johnny Ciao's
    Opera Mix (see page 136
    for substitutions)

1/4 cup (1 oz.) shredded
    mozzarella cheese

2 tablespoons plain fine bread
    crumbs

1 1/2 cup virgin olive oil

*M*ix together all ingredients except bread crumbs and oil in a large bowl. Form mixture into ice cream scoop–size balls. Place bread crumbs in a shallow bowl. Coat each rice ball with bread crumbs.

*H*eat oil in a heavy skillet or saucepan to 375F (190C). Add balls, in batches, and fry until golden brown, about 10 minutes. Drain on paper towels. Serve hot.

BLUESY BURRITO

2 tablespoons olive oil

3 jalapeño chiles, minced

4 medium white onions, chopped

3 yellow or red bell peppers, chopped

2 pounds lean ground beef

2 tablespoons Johnny Ciao's BarBQ Blues (see page 136 for substitutions)

1 teaspoon Worcestershire sauce

2 cups (8 oz.) shredded Cheddar or Jack cheese

16 whole-wheat or white flour tortillas, warmed

*P*reheat oven to 375F (190C). Grease a baking sheet with sides. Heat olive oil in a medium skillet over medium heat. Add chiles, onions and bell peppers; sauté 3 minutes or until onion is softened. Transfer vegetables to a bowl with a slotted spoon and set aside. Add beef to skillet. Cook, stirring to break up meat, until beef is browned. Add Johnny Ciao's BarBQ Blues, Worcestershire sauce and reserved vegetables; cook, stirring occasionally, until hot. Drain.

*S*poon equal amount of mixture onto one edge of each tortilla. Sprinkle with cheese and carefully roll, tucking ends under so that mixture does not spill out. Place seam side down on baking sheet. Bake 15 minutes. Cut into thirds and serve hot.

*T*here are days when I find myself feeding hundreds of mouths at the same time. From appearances at department stores to festivals to trade shows, I've come up with inventive hand-cut rolls for these occasions that can be served as appetizers. You can also freeze them for future bites.

ZUCCHINI SUSHI DRUM ROLLS

Since so many people are turned off by the thought of eating raw fish, try this creative alternative.

10 medium to large zucchini

1/4 cup virgin olive oil

3 cloves garlic, minced

4 whole green onions, minced

2 large Portobello mushrooms, chopped

1 teaspoon Johnny Ciao's Country Herbs (see page 136 for substitutions)

1 pound shrimp, shelled and deveined

2 tablespoons plain fine bread crumbs

2 eggs, beaten

1 (8-oz.) can tomato puree

2 tablespoons prepared wasabi (optional)

Rice to serve (optional)

*P*reheat oven to 350F (175C). Remove centers from each zucchini with an apple corer, then brush with a little of the olive oil. Place in casserole dishes and bake 15 to 20 minutes or until medium-soft; do *not* overcook. Let cool.

*H*eat remaining olive oil in a medium skillet over medium heat. Add garlic and onions; sauté 2 minutes. Add mushrooms, cover and cook 3 minutes. Add herbs and cook for several minutes, then add shrimp and cook 1 minute. Let cool.

*F*inely chop vegetable-shrimp mixture either in a food processor or with a knife. If using a food processor, add bread crumbs and eggs, and process until combined. If chopping with a knife, transfer chopped mixture to a bowl and stir in bread crumbs and eggs, mixing well. Spoon mixture into centers of each zucchini. Return stuffed zucchini to baking pan and pour tomato puree over zucchini. Bake 30 minutes. Remove and slice into 3/4- to 1-inch-thick slices. Top off with a dab of wasabi, if using. Serve with rice, if desired.

ZUCCHINI FLOWERS WITH GINGER LIME DIP

12 to 15 whole baby zucchini
with flowers attached

2 eggs, beaten

1/4 cup milk

1/4 cup whole-wheat flour

2 teaspoons Johnny Ciao's
Opera Mix (see page 136
for substitutions)

1/2 cup virgin olive oil

Ginger Lime Dip (page 110)

Take whole baby zucchini and carefully slice down the center of the vegetable, leaving the flower intact. Set aside. In a large bowl, mix eggs and milk, then slowly sprinkle in flour and Johnny Ciao's Opera Mix until a thin batter is formed. Carefully batter each zucchini and flower, then refrigerate on a baking sheet for 15 minutes.

Heat oil in medium skillet over medium-high heat. Add zucchini, in batches, and quickly brown on both sides. Drain excess oil on paper towels. Place on your favorite party platter and serve warm with Ginger Lime Dip.

When most people see flowers on the ends of certain vegetables, they don't seem to get as excited as I do. The taste and nutritional value far exceed what you get from the vegetable itself, and coming up with new ways to prepare edible flowers is exciting and challenging. One of my favorites is the baby zucchini flower, which is only available throughout the summer months. Its vibrant orange/green color looks great on the plate.

Raven-Symone and friend chow down on Johnny's Vegtaballs at Atlanta's Celebrity Rock Cafe.

VEGTABALLS

2 cups broccoli or other greens, cooked until soft

1/3 cup all-purpose flour

2/3 cup plain fine bread crumbs

2 eggs, beaten

1/4 cup freshly grated Parmesan cheese

1/4 cup shredded Monterey Jack cheese

2 tablespoons chopped walnuts

10 flat-leaf parsley sprigs, finely chopped

2 teaspoons Johnny Ciao's Country Herbs (see page 136 for substitutions)

1 cup canola oil

Drummin' Dips and Dressings (pages 107–20) to serve

In a large bowl, mash broccoli. Add flour, bread crumbs, eggs, cheeses, walnuts, parsley and herbs. Mix until a dough with a sticky consistency is formed.

Heat oil in a heavy saucepan or deep-fryer to 375F (190C). Form 1/4 cup of mixture into balls and add, in batches, to hot oil. Fry until golden brown on all sides, about 10 minutes. Drain on paper towels. Serve hot with one of the Drummin' Dips and Dressings as an accompaniment.

As a child I ate everything Mom put in front of me, including green vegetables. But we all know how difficult it can be to get most kids to eat spinach, broccoli, asparagus, zucchini and other green veggies. This is a great way to get kids—and adults—to eat their greens.

Symphonic Soups and Salads

OLD-FASHIONED HEN SOUP

2 (3- to 4-lb.) hens (stewing
  chickens)

8 cups water

1 leek, chopped

6 carrots, sliced into 1-inch-
  thick pieces

3 celery stalks, chopped

2 tablespoons chopped flat-
  leaf parsley

2 teaspoons kosher salt

1/4 cup tomato puree

Rinse hens and pat dry with paper towels. Remove and discard any excess fat. Place hens and all remaining ingredients in a stockpot over medium heat. Bring to a boil and skim off any foam that forms. Reduce heat to low, cover and simmer 2 hours or until hens are tender.

Remove hens from stockpot; cool enough to handle. Remove skin and bones and cut meat into bite-size pieces. Skim off any surface fat and return meat to stockpot. Serve in soup bowls.

Making good chicken soup is a real art, but one that can be perfected with a bit of practice and a few tricks of the trade. I particularly like using hens, as they contain less fat than younger chickens. It's important to soak the hens in salt water for several hours prior to cooking.

BLACK BEAN SOUP

Black beans are a good and inexpensive source of fiber. With the strong influence of Latin American cooking, black bean soup has become a favorite in North America. Here is a simple version of my favorite southwestern style black bean soup.

2 pounds black beans, soaked overnight and drained
3 cloves garlic, minced
4 carrots, peeled and chopped
2 celery stalks, chopped
8 cilantro sprigs, chopped
1 bay leaf
1 large red onion, chopped
1 tablespoon Johnny Ciao's Soulful Seafood (see page 136 for substitutions)
1 teaspoon cumin powder
Sour cream to garnish
Lime wedges to garnish

Combine beans, garlic, carrots, celery, cilantro, bay leaf, onion, Johnny Ciao's Soulful Seafood and cumin in a large stockpot with enough water to cover; boil 10 minutes over medium-high heat. Reduce heat, cover and simmer 90 minutes or until beans are tender, adding more water if needed.

Discard bay leaf. Remove 2 cups beans from pot and puree in a food processor or blender. Return pureed beans to pot and simmer 30 minutes, stirring occasionally. Serve hot in bowls with a dollop of sour cream and a squeeze of lime juice.

CARROT GINGER VICHYSSOISE

2 tablespoons virgin olive oil

1 clove garlic, minced

1 thin slice gingerroot

1 leek (white part only),
   washed and sliced

8 medium carrots, chopped
   into large pieces

2 medium potatoes, peeled
   and chopped into large
   pieces

2 bay leaves

8 cups (64 oz.) chicken broth

1 teaspoon salt

1 teaspoon Johnny Ciao's
   Country Herbs (see page
   136 for substitutions)

1/2 teaspoon dried dill weed

1 cup whipping cream or low-
   fat sour cream

Chives, lime peel or a dollop of
   sour cream or yogurt
   to garnish

This is one of those great soups that you can eat either cold or hot. It's a real comfort food with a zing.

Heat olive oil in a large pot over low heat. Add garlic and gingerroot and cook until soft. Add leeks, increase heat to medium-low and cook until the leeks begin to wilt, about 10 minutes. Add the carrots, potatoes, bay leaves, chicken broth, salt, dill and herbs, and bring to a boil. Reduce heat and simmer 20 minutes, or until all vegetables are soft.

Discard bay leaves. Cool, then puree the soup in a blender at low speed until very smooth; return soup to pot. Add the cream and adjust salt. Pour into storage container and refrigerate until chilled. Serve soup in chilled soup bowls. Garnish with chives, lime peel or a dollop of sour cream or yogurt.

ESCAROLE AND BEAN SOUP

2 tablespoons virgin olive oil

2 cloves garlic, minced

1 1/2 teaspoons capers, chopped

2 cups water

2 (15-oz.) cans cannellini beans, drained

1/2 teaspoon salt

2 heads escarole, washed, trimmed, chopped into large pieces

*W*hen I was growing up, one of my favorite soup dishes was always escarole with cannellini (white kidney) beans. It's so simple to prepare, costs practically nothing, and is loaded with vitamins and fiber.

*H*eat olive oil in a large pot over medium heat. Add garlic and capers and sauté 1 minute. Add water, cannellini beans and salt. Bring to a boil and boil 3 minutes. Add escarole. Reduce heat to low and simmer 15 minutes or until escarole is tender. Serve hot.

PUMPKIN LEEK SOUP

1 medium pumpkin (about 6 lbs.)

4 tablespoons unsalted butter

2 tablespoons virgin olive oil

2 large leeks, chopped

2 quarts chicken broth, warmed

1/2 cup dry white wine

2 teaspoons salt

2 teaspoons Johnny Ciao's
   Country Herbs (see page
   136 for substitutions)

2 limes, zested and juiced

1/2 cup sour cream

Preheat oven to 400F (205C). Cut the pumpkin in half and remove strings and seeds. Place in a baking dish, cut sides down, and cover bottom of pan with water. Bake 45 minutes or until tender when pierced with a fork. Let pumpkin stand until cool enough to handle and scrape pumpkin flesh from shell with a spoon to make about 6 cups.

Spread pumpkin seeds in a single layer on a baking sheet. Sprinkle with salt and bake about 3 minutes or until slightly browned. Set aside.

In a large skillet, heat the butter and oil over medium heat. Add leeks and sauté until soft, about 10 minutes. Add 1 cup of the chicken broth. Reduce heat to low, cover and simmer about 10 minutes, then remove from heat. In a deep stockpot, heat the remaining chicken broth over low heat.

In a blender or food processor, puree the pumpkin flesh in small batches, slowly adding the hot chicken broth to liquefy. Return blended pumpkin flesh to the stockpot and stir. Then add the sautéed leek mixture, wine, salt, and the Johnny Ciao's Country Herbs. Simmer slowly for an additional 30 minutes.

In a small bowl, combine the lime juice and sour cream. Drizzle this mixture over soup in bowls, then sprinkle with pumpkin seeds and lime zest for garnish.

When television producer Bill Bell bought the old Howard Hughes estate in the hills above Hollywood, I created this seasonal dish for the housewarming party. I served the soup in mini-pumpkins. This recipe takes a little patience to prepare, but is well worth the effort.

*M*ost people don't relish the thought of cooking or eating hot food —except off the barbecue—during the hot summer months. This simple yet classic fruit soup will pick up any appetite, even in the dog days of August.

PEARBERRY SOUP

3 pears, peeled, cored and chopped

1 1/4 cups raspberries

1/4 teaspoon ground cinnamon

1 1/2 cups cranberry juice

Yogurt to garnish

*C*ombine pears, 1 cup raspberries, cinnamon and cranberry juice in a blender or food processor. Process until pureed. Pour into a bowl, cover and refrigerate until chilled. Pour into bowls and serve cold garnished with remaining whole raspberries and yogurt.

DIXIELAND TOMATO BISQUE

1 (16-oz.) can whole tomatoes

1 cup nonfat yogurt

1/4 teaspoon hot pepper sauce

2 cloves garlic, minced

1 teaspoon prepared horseradish

Jalapeño chile, minced, and 2
   tablespoons lemon zest to
   garnish (optional)

Combine tomatoes, yogurt, hot pepper sauce, garlic and horseradish in a blender or food processor; process until pureed. Pour mixture into a bowl, cover and refrigerate until chilled. Pour into bowls and serve cold garnished with minced chile and lemon zest, if desired.

This relative of gazpacho, the tangy cold Spanish soup, requires no culinary skills whatsoever to prepare. The only effort will be helping yourself to seconds.

MOM'S ZUCCHINI SOUP

4 medium zucchini, diced

1 large white onion, chopped

2 medium potatoes, diced

1/4 cup virgin olive oil

10 flat-leaf parsley sprigs,
   chopped

1 (10-oz.) package frozen green
   peas

1 tablespoon Johnny Ciao's
   Opera Mix (see page 136
   for substitutions)

1/2 cup water

1 cup cooked white rice

Combine zucchini, onion, potatoes, olive oil, parsley, peas, Johnny Ciao's Opera Mix and water in a medium stockpot. Cover and cook over low heat 45 minutes, stirring occasionally. Add rice and heat until hot. Serve hot.

My mom has a soup for every kind of vegetable that exists, from asparagus to broccoli to cauliflower to zucchini. Most of these soups are simple to prepare and extremely good for your body as well as your soul. Even if you're not a zucchini fan, you are guaranteed to love this combination of ingredients.

POP SALAD

Mixed greens (red leaf, chicories, endive, radicchio, butter, etc.) for 4 servings
2 tablespoons walnut oil
1 peach, peeled, pitted and chopped
1 pear, peeled, cored and chopped
1 apple, peeled, cored and chopped
Fresh lemon juice
1/4 cup fresh raspberries
1/4 cup chopped walnuts
4 ounces Gorgonzola cheese, crumbled

*J*f you like fruit, then this salad will blow you and your guests away. It's simple to prepare, and contains great texture and flavor. Allow the fruit to sit in the walnut oil and cheese for 10 minutes to enrich the flavor.

*A*rrange greens in a salad bowl. Drizzle walnut oil over greens and toss gently to combine. Combine peach, pear and apple with lemon juice. Add to greens and toss gently. Top with raspberries, walnuts and cheese.

Variation
Combine fruit, walnut oil and cheese and let stand 20 minutes before tossing with greens. This will enhance the overall flavor.

Composer/Pianist George Michalski (left) and Bob Weir of the
Grateful Dead (center) joined Johnny backstage at his
Performance Cuisine party.

PSYCHEDELIC BEAN SALAD

6 cups black beans, cooked
and drained

1 medium green bell pepper,
finely chopped

1 medium yellow green pepper,
finely chopped

1 medium red bell pepper,
finely chopped

1 large red onion, finely
chopped

2 jalapeño chiles, minced

1 cup diced jicama root

1 teaspoon cumin seeds

1 teaspoon Johnny Ciao's
Soulful Seafood (see page
136 for substitutions)

1/4 cup white wine vinegar

1/2 cup cilantro-infused olive
oil or plain olive oil

10 sprigs fresh cilantro, finely
chopped

Combine all ingredients in a large bowl. Toss gently to combine. Cover and refrigerate 1 to 4 hours. Serve chilled.

Although I've prepared a wide range of dishes for rock stars, sometimes I look for a special "backstage" recipe that provides lots of protein and vitamins for that high-energy performance. You know how much energy a rocker needs on stage. This recipe has provided that extra voltage for Carlos Santana, Huey Lewis, and the Grateful Dead. It can be prepared in advance, leaving much-needed time the day of the show.

POTATO MUSSEL SALAD

*T*ired of the same old potato salads? Then try this unusual combination. If you like mussels, you'll make this one of your regular dishes.

8 to 10 small new red or white potatoes, cooked just until tender and cooled

1 pound mussels, cleaned, steamed and shelled (see page 6)

3 tablespoons virgin olive oil

2 cloves garlic, minced

1 red onion, chopped

1 celery stalk, finely chopped

8 flat-leaf parsley sprigs, minced

1 tablespoon balsamic vinegar

1 teaspoon Johnny Ciao's Opera Mix (see page 136 for substitutions)

*C*ut potatoes into medium-size cubes and refrigerate. Cover and refrigerate mussels.

*H*eat olive oil in a medium skillet over medium heat. Add garlic, onion, celery and parsley and sauté until softened, about 5 minutes. Pour sautéed mixture over chilled potatoes. Add vinegar, Johnny Ciao's Opera Mix and mussels, then toss together. Serve immediately or cover and refrigerate until well chilled.

STING BEAN SALAD

8 to 10 red or white new
   potatoes
1/2 pound green beans
2 medium white onions
1/4 cup virgin olive oil
2 tablespoons balsamic
   vinegar

1 to 2 teaspoons Johnny Ciao's
   Country Herbs (see page
   136 for substitutions)
2 tablespoons pine nuts,
   toasted (see Note)

This salad is a wonderful side dish or great on its own! It holds up well in the refrigerator for two days.

Cook potatoes in a large saucepan of boiling salted water 10 minutes. Add beans and onions and cook 15 minutes or until potatoes are tender and beans are crisp-tender. Drain and rinse vegetables with cold water. Transfer to a salad bowl, cover and refrigerate 15 minutes or more. Toss with oil, vinegar, Johnny Ciao's Country Herbs and pine nuts.

Note

Toast pine nuts in a heavy skillet over low heat about 5 minutes, stirring often, or spread on a baking sheet and toast in a 350F (175C) oven, watching carefully, about 5 minutes.

Pasta Percussions

AGLIO E OLIO CON VERDURA

1/4 cup virgin olive oil

4 cloves garlic, minced

1 medium zucchini, sliced

1/4 cup water

1 cup lightly packed fresh
    spinach, chopped

1 teaspoon Johnny Ciao's
    Opera Mix (see page 136
    for substitutions)

1 tablespoon chopped flat-leaf
    parsley

1 pound pasta of choice,
    cooked and drained

Freshly grated Parmesan or
    Romano cheese to serve

*H*eat oil in a medium skillet over medium heat. Add garlic and sauté 1 minute. Add zucchini and sauté 2 minutes. Add water and spinach and cook 3 minutes. Add Johnny Ciao's Opera Mix and parsley, reduce heat to low and cook 3 minutes or until vegetables are tender. Pour sauce over pasta in a large bowl and add cheese. Toss to combine.

*E*veryone seems to love the taste, smell and flavor of garlic—a fact that is no less true of *aglio e olio* ("garlic and oil"), one of the simplest pasta garlic dishes to prepare. I've taken this tasty dish and added some green vegetables to give it more dimension and flavor.

The late comedienne Minnie Pearl and Johnny shared an interest in great Italian food. In her signature straw hat and gingham apron, Minnie was ready to give a hand in the kitchen.

NEW AGE PASTA FAGIOLA

2 tablespoons virgin olive oil

2 cloves garlic, minced

1 small white onion, chopped

3 medium carrots, diced

1 cup water or vegetable stock

1 yellow or green summer squash, diced

2 medium tomatoes, peeled and chopped

2 (15-oz.) cans cannellini beans, drained

1 teaspoon Johnny Ciao's Opera Mix (see page 136 for substitutions)

6 to 8 flat-leaf parsley sprigs, chopped

1 pound tubettini pasta, cooked and drained

Heat olive oil in a small stockpot over low heat. Add garlic and onion and sauté until soft, about 5 minutes. Add carrots and 1/2 cup of the water. Cover and cook over medium heat 3 minutes. Add squash, tomatoes, cannellini beans and Johnny Ciao's Opera Mix and cook over low heat 10 minutes, adding additional water if mixture is too dry. Add parsley and cook 5 minutes. Add pasta and toss to combine.

This is one of those classic Italian peasant dishes that I've always enjoyed. It's hearty and tasty. I've added vegetables to the mix to boost the fiber, nutrition and taste. It tastes even better the next day.

FARFALLE PORCINI

*M*ost porcini mushrooms found in this country are dried, but with a bit of water, oil or sherry, you can transform them into mouth-watering delicacies. While they might appear to be expensive, a very few go a long way.

2 tablespoons dried porcini
   mushrooms
2 tablespoons virgin olive oil
1 large shallot, chopped
1 yellow bell pepper, finely
   sliced
1 celery stalk, finely chopped
2 medium tomatoes, peeled
   and chopped
1 cup (1/2 pint) whipping
   cream
10 flat-leaf parsley sprigs,
   chopped
1 pound farfalle or bow-tie
   pasta, cooked and drained
1/4 cup freshly grated
   Parmesan or Romano
   cheese to serve

*S*oak porcini mushrooms in water to cover 1 hour. Drain mushrooms, reserving liquid, and cut into fine strips. Heat olive oil in a medium saucepan over medium heat. Add shallot, bell pepper and celery and sauté until soft, about 5 minutes. Add tomatoes, mushroom strips and reserved liquid. Cover and cook 5 minutes over medium heat. Reduce heat to low and add cream and parsley. Simmer, stirring often, 5 minutes or until slightly thickened. Pour sauce over pasta in a large bowl and add cheese. Toss to combine.

COLD PASTA PRIMAVERA

1/4 cup virgin olive oil

2 cloves garlic, minced

1 small red onion, sliced

1 medium yellow squash,
diced

10 small cherry tomatoes, cut
in half

10 flat-leaf parsley sprigs,
chopped

1 tablespoon pine nuts

1 lemon, cut into slices

1 pound fusilli, ziti or any
shaped macaroni, cooked
and drained

1/4 cup freshly grated
Parmesan or Romano
cheese

Heat olive oil in a large skillet over medium heat. Add garlic and onion and sauté 1 minute. Add yellow squash and cherry tomatoes. Cover and cook 3 minutes, then add parsley, pine nuts and lemon slices. Cook, covered, 2 minutes. Pour sauce over pasta in a large bowl and add cheese. Toss to combine. Serve at room temperature or cover and refrigerate up to 24 hours.

I spent some time in San Francisco, where the late rock promoter Bill Graham hired me to work alongside the Hard Rock Cafe hospitality booth at the Annual Bay Area Music Awards. I had to make enough pasta salad to feed a thousand rockers, their friends, members of the media, and whomever. I didn't have any real catering experience at the time and cooked way too much. We donated the rest to feed the homeless.

In a much scaled-down version, here's what I made for the Award Show that first year.

PASTA CREAMAVERA

I've always loved pasta with cream sauces. But even before reports came out cautioning us about the danger of eating heavy cream sauces, I always looked for alternative ways to capture the flavor and texture of those rich and delicious pasta dishes.

1/4 cup virgin olive oil

2 cloves garlic, minced

1 teaspoon minced gingerroot

1/2 red onion, thinly sliced

2 small carrots, sliced

1 medium zucchini, sliced

1/2 cup sliced mushrooms

2 tablespoons finely chopped
   fresh parsley

1/4 cup low-fat sour cream

1 pound macaroni of choice,
   cooked and drained

2 tablespoons freshly grated
   Parmesan or Romano
   cheese to serve

*H*eat olive oil in a large skillet over medium heat. Add garlic, gingerroot and onion and sauté 2 minutes. Add carrots, cover and cook 5 minutes or until carrots soften. Add zucchini and mushrooms and cook, uncovered, 5 minutes or until zucchini is crisp-tender. Reduce heat to low, stir in parsley and sour cream. Cook 2 minutes, then pour sauce over pasta in a large bowl. Add cheese and toss to combine.

PINK SHELLFISH PASTA

2 tablespoons virgin olive oil

2 cloves garlic, minced

4 medium tomatoes, peeled and chopped

1/2 teaspoon red pepper flakes

1/2 teaspoon saffron threads

1 dozen medium clams, rinsed

1 pound mussels, rinsed, beards removed

1/2 pound medium shrimp, shelled and deveined

1/2 pound sea scallops

1 pound linguine, cooked and drained

Heat olive oil in a medium saucepan over medium heat. Add garlic and sauté 1 minute. Add tomatoes and pepper flakes, cover and cook 5 minutes or until tomatoes are soft. Reduce heat to low and add saffron threads, clams and mussels. Cook, covered, until clam and mussel shells open. Discard any clams or mussels that remain closed. Add shrimp and scallops and cook 2 minutes or until shrimp are pink and scallops are opaque. Pour sauce over linguine in a large bowl and toss to combine.

I love linguine with clams or mussels or shrimp, and sometimes I mix a variety of shellfish for maximum taste. My pink shellfish sauce is a bit lighter and, I believe, tastier than the traditional version. Let's take that oldie but goodie and remix it. See for yourself which version is "more happening."

PASTA ALLA GRATTE

This is a classic Neapolitan dish that my dad, Pasquale, prepares, whenever he's allowed in the kitchen. Mom has a thing about letting anyone cook in her kitchen, except me, of course.

1 pound rigatoni pasta

1/4 cup virgin olive oil

2 medium onions, chopped

3 eggs, lightly beaten

1 cup (4 oz.) shredded
  mozzarella cheese

2 tablespoons grated
  Romano cheese

10 flat-leaf parsley sprigs,
  chopped

4 oz. prosciutto, chopped

Cook pasta in boiling water until al dente. Drain and reserve 1/4 cup cooking water. Set pasta and water aside.

Preheat oven to 375F (190C). Grease a deep medium baking dish. Turn pasta into prepared dish.

Heat olive oil in a large skillet over medium heat. Add onions and sauté 3 minutes or until softened. Add water from pasta. Slowly stir in eggs; don't scramble. Remove mixture from heat. Add cheeses, parsley and prosciutto to the egg mixture. Pour egg mixture over pasta and stir to combine. Bake 30 minutes, gently stirring several times, or until heated through. Let cool 5 minutes, then serve hot.

SPAGHETTI PUTANESCA

1/4 cup virgin olive oil

2 cloves garlic, minced

1 teaspoon capers, minced

5 anchovy fillets

4 to 6 black Gaeta olives,
    pitted and minced

2 tablespoons freshly
    chopped parsley

2 medium tomatoes, peeled
    and chopped

1 pound spaghetti, cooked
    and drained

Heat olive oil in a medium skillet over medium-low heat. Add garlic, capers, anchovies, olives, parsley and tomatoes. Cover and cook, stirring occasionally, about 15 minutes, until ingredients soften and blend together. Pour sauce over spaghetti in a large bowl and toss to combine.

There were a couple of entertainment executives who visited me for lunch on a regular basis while I was living in the Hollywood Hills, and they just loved the taste of anchovies. Here's one of their favorites, as well as mine. Don't overdo the amount of anchovies, and please no additional salt in this dish, or you'll have a sodium attack.

SALMON BASILICO

The combination of flavors here is awesome. I know you'll agree.

2 tablespoons virgin olive oil

2 cloves garlic, minced

2 teaspoons capers, minced

4 Roma tomatoes, peeled and chopped

1 teaspoon Johnny Ciao's Opera Mix (see page 136 for substitutions)

1/2 pound oyster mushrooms, thinly sliced

1 (1-lb.) salmon filet

6 to 8 fresh basil leaves, chopped

1 pound spaghetti, cooked and drained

Heat olive oil in a large skillet over medium heat. Add garlic and capers and sauté 1 minute. Add tomatoes, Johnny Ciao's Opera Mix and mushrooms. Cook over medium heat 3 minutes. Place salmon in pan, skin side up. Reduce heat, cover and cook 5 minutes or until salmon turns from translucent to opaque. Remove salmon skin with a fork and add basil. Break up salmon into large chunks, blending with sauce. Pour sauce over pasta in a large bowl and toss to combine.

SHROOM AND SHALLOT CHICKEN PASTA

2 tablespoons virgin olive oil

2 cloves garlic, finely chopped

2 shallots, chopped

2 whole boneless skinless
    chicken breasts, sliced

1 teaspoon pure ground chiles

1/4 pound shiitake mushrooms,
    thinly sliced

1/4 pound white button
    mushrooms, thinly sliced

1 teaspoon Johnny Ciao's
    Rockin' Poultry (see page
    136 for substitutions)

1 rosemary sprig

1 pound pasta of choice,
    cooked and drained

Heat olive oil in a large skillet over medium heat. Add garlic and shallots and sauté 1 minute. Add sliced chicken and cook, turning, until brown on all sides, about 5 minutes. Reduce heat and add ground chiles, mushrooms and Johnny Ciao's Rockin' Poultry Mix. Cover and cook 5 minutes, then add rosemary and cook 3 minutes or until chicken is tender. Pour sauce over pasta in a large bowl and toss to combine.

This is one rockin' pasta dish. Keep it covered in order to yield extra liquid for your pasta. You could pour the sauce over the pasta and bake it in the oven, adding a soft grated cheese to the top for an extra beat.

*E*very Italian family has a big meal on Sunday, and each has their own special kind of red sauce or marinara sauce, or as I call it, Sunday Sauce. It's a classic Italian thick tomato sauce that generally takes hours of slow dancing in the kitchen. Blended with love, tender care and lots of shouting, most Italian families observe the tradition of preparing a Sunday Sauce every week.

Sunday Sauce can sometimes take several attempts before getting it right. Don't get disheartened, because once you've perfected your version of Sunday Sauce, it will become your family tradition.

This recipe is also used in preparing other dishes in this book.

SUNDAY SAUCE

2 tablespoons virgin olive oil
2 cloves garlic, minced
1 medium onion, finely chopped
2 (28-oz.) cans imported whole peeled tomatoes
1 (8-oz.) can tomato paste

1/3 cup water
2 tablespoons Johnny Ciao's Opera Mix (see page 136 for substitutions)
10 fresh basil leaves
8 flat-leaf parsley sprigs, chopped

*H*eat olive oil in a deep nonaluminum pot over medium-low heat. Add garlic and onion and sauté 1 minute. In a blender or food processor, process tomatoes, tomato paste, water and Johnny Ciao's Opera Mix until smooth, then add to pot. Cook, stirring occasionally, 1 hour over low heat. Add basil and parsley and cook 15 to 20 minutes or until sauce is thickened. Turn heat off and let sit 20 minutes.

Variations

When making meatballs in sauce or adding meat to make a meat sauce, the browned meatballs or meat should be added to the sauce after it has cooked 45 minutes. The meatballs or meat should be undercooked when browned to withstand additional cooking time in the sauce. This is the secret to creating tasty meat dishes in Sunday Sauce.

If tomatoes are too bitter, then add a little sugar to the sauce.

Rockin' Poultry

CIAO'S CREAMY LIGHT TURKEY

2 tablespoons virgin olive oil

1 small leek, chopped

1 celery stalk, chopped

3 Roma tomatoes, peeled and chopped

1 tablespoon cornstarch

1/4 cup skim milk

1/2 cup chicken broth

3 to 4 cups (1/2-inch pieces) turkey or chicken leftovers

10 flour tortillas, warmed

1/2 cup (2 oz.) shredded Monterey Jack or Cheddar cheese

Never let good food go to waste. Try this recipe with your chicken or turkey leftovers.

Heat oil in a medium skillet over medium heat. Add leek and celery and sauté 5 minutes. Add tomatoes, cover and cook 3 minutes or until vegetables are softened. In a small bowl, mix together cornstarch, milk and broth. Add turkey or chicken to skillet with vegetables and stir in cornstarch mixture. Reduce heat and cook, stirring, until mixture thickens, about 5 minutes. Serve in flour tortillas with shredded cheese.

*Y*ou know that screaming sound generated by an electric guitar? This chicken dish produces similar gustatory waves when you eat it.

ELECTRIFYING CHICKEN BREASTS

1 jalapeño chile, seeded and minced

2 tablespoons Dijon mustard

2 tablespoons orange marmalade

2 teaspoons fresh lime juice

1 teaspoon dried mint leaves

1 tablespoon virgin olive oil

2 teaspoons chopped Gaeta or other ripe olives

4 skinless boneless chicken breast halves, rinsed

*C*ombine chile, mustard, marmalade, lime juice, mint leaves, olive oil and olives in a shallow baking dish that can go from refrigerator to oven. Add chicken to dish and marinate in mixture 1 hour at room temperature or overnight in the refrigerator, turning chicken occasionally.

*P*reheat oven to 350F (175C). Bake 25 minutes or until chicken is cooked through, basting with cooking juices at least once during cooking time. Add some water to the dish if it becomes too dry. Serve with one of the vegetable dishes from Veggie Vocals (pages 95–105).

OATMEAL CHICKEN BREASTS

2 tablespoons virgin olive oil

1/2 cup rolled oats

2 tablespoons dry bread
    crumbs

2 tablespoons blue corn flour

2 eggs, beaten

4 skinless chicken breast
    halves, rinsed

Caramelized Onions (page
    100) to serve

*P*reheat oven to 375F (190C). Pour olive oil into a baking dish large enough to hold chicken in a single layer. Mix oatmeal, bread crumbs and corn flour in a large bowl. Put beaten eggs in another bowl. Coat chicken with oat mixture, then dip into eggs, covering chicken well. Return chicken to the oat mixture once again and coat evenly. Place chicken in the baking dish. Bake 30 minutes or until chicken is browned. Serve with onions.

*T*he first time I met Whitney Houston was at Michael Jackson's Neverland Valley. She came up to spend the day, and before we saddled our horses to ride into unknown territory on the ranch, we ate. Whitney requested fried chicken, so I prepared it with a different spin. Everyone loves fried chicken, but these days most of us are shying away from fried anything. Here's a recipe that will give you that same fried chicken flavor, without the frying, and I know you'll enjoy it as much as Whitney did.

BAKED ORIENTAL CHICKEN

*H*ere's another quick-and-easy dish that can be prepared the night before. If you have one hectic schedule, have to wake up early, maybe get the kids off to school, and then go to work yourself, this recipe will help. If you prepare it and marinate the chicken the night before, you'll have it real easy when you get home from work. Just pop it in the oven and eat!

1/2 cup low-sodium soy sauce

2 teaspoons brown sugar

1/2 cup rice wine

1 tablespoon sesame oil

2 teaspoons chopped
    gingerroot

2 green onions, finely chopped

4 skinless boneless chicken
    breast halves, rinsed

Cooked rice to serve

*C*ombine soy sauce, brown sugar, rice wine, sesame oil, gingerroot and green onions in a shallow baking dish that can go from refrigerator to oven. Add chicken to dish and marinate in the mixture 1 hour at room temperature or overnight in the refrigerator, turning chicken occasionally.

*P*reheat oven to 350F (175C). Bake 25 minutes or until chicken is cooked through, basting with cooking juices at least once during cooking time. Place chicken on plates and pour cooking juices over chicken. Serve with rice.

RADICCHIO CHICKEN TACOS

2 tablespoons virgin olive oil, plus extra for brushing

1/2 pound boneless, skinless chicken, cut into bite-size chunks

2 cloves garlic, minced

2 green onions, chopped

1/4 pound Portobello mushrooms, chopped

1 teaspoon Johnny Ciao Opera Mix (see page 136 for substitutions)

1 small to medium head of radicchio

2 tablespoons shredded mozzarella cheese

Preheat oven to 375F (190C). Heat olive oil in a medium skillet over medium heat. Add chicken and sauté until browned on all sides, turning. Remove chicken with a slotted spoon and drain on paper towels. Add garlic and green onions to drippings in skillet. Cook over medium heat 2 minutes. Add mushrooms and Johnny Ciao Opera Mix and cook 3 minutes. Return browned chicken to skillet and stir to combine. Cook 2 minutes. Drain chicken mixture in a strainer and place in a bowl.

Separate and rinse radicchio leaves, then pat dry with paper towels. Brush each leaf lightly with olive oil and place on a baking sheet. Carefully place a spoonful of chicken mixture in each leaf, then sprinkle with mozzarella cheese. Bake 10 minutes or until cheese melts.

Radicchio is a member of the rich, red chicory family, and is usually mixed into salads with other chicories and greens. It can also be brushed with olive oil and grilled in chunks, or used as a taco shell, as I have here.

STUFFED TURKEY ROTOLO

MAKES 4 TO 6 SERVINGS

*H*ere's another oldie but goodie recipe. My family used to prepare chopped meat *braciola*, which is ground beef delicately rolled with spices and herbs, then placed in a thick red Sunday Sauce (see page 46). It simmers for hours in the sauce, to create a delicious dish. I took the traditional recipe and flipped Grandma out with a hipper version. Check out this remake of an old classic.

1 pound ground turkey

3 eggs

1/2 cup fine plain bread crumbs

1/2 yellow bell pepper, finely chopped

2 tablespoons chopped flat-leaf parsley

2 tablespoons pine nuts

1/2 cup chopped fresh spinach leaves

1 tablespoon Johnny Ciao Opera Mix (see page 136 for substitutions)

1 tablespoon virgin olive oil

1 recipe Sunday Sauce (page 46)

*M*ix 1 egg into ground turkey in a medium bowl. Divide meat into 6 equal portions. Spread each one out on a large sheet of waxed paper and flatten into a 4-inch square.

*B*eat remaining 2 eggs in a medium bowl. Stir in bread crumbs, bell pepper, parsley, pine nuts, spinach and Johnny Ciao Opera Mix. Place a spoonful of stuffing mixture onto each ground turkey square and spread evenly. Using wax paper underneath, carefully roll each ground turkey square, removing waxed paper as you roll. Tuck in ends so that stuffing doesn't fall out.

*H*eat olive oil in a large skillet over high heat. Add turkey rolls and brown quickly on all sides, turning. Remove from pan and immediately lower into simmering Sunday Sauce. Simmer 1 hour. Carefully remove turkey rolls from sauce and cut each roll into 4 to 6 slices. Serve with sauce.

SICILIAN HENS IN MACHINE GUN BROTH

2 tablespoons virgin olive oil

3 cloves garlic, minced

1 small onion, chopped

2 Cornish game hens, rinsed

1 bell pepper, chopped

8 whole Roma tomatoes,
    peeled and chopped

10 ounces button mushrooms,
    sliced

2 cups water

1 tablespoon dried oregano

1 teaspoon dried rosemary

1 dash cayenne pepper or to
    taste

2 teaspoons large capers

Heat olive oil in a large pot over medium heat. Add garlic and onion and sauté until softened. Add chicken, bell pepper, tomatoes, mushrooms, water, oregano, rosemary, cayenne and capers. Reduce heat to low, cover and simmer 1 hour or until hens are tender. Cut hens in half and serve.

In our close-knit Italian family, my grandmother was always in the kitchen. Every once in a while I'd sneak in to watch her cook, and sometimes play tricks on her—fake mice, rubber unmentionables, etc. One day I went too far.

Grandma was cooking some freshly killed chickens in a *cacciatore* sauce. While the birds were cooking, Grandma visited my Aunt Jean next door, and I went to work. I climbed up on a chair, took the lid off the chicken pot and neatly placed little plastic machine guns on the birds. As I was climbing down, guess who walked in? Grandma grabbed my two hands and banged them against each other, and then against my face. Then she noticed the machine guns floating in the pot, and sparks flew louder than the sound of any real machine gun. This dish is dedicated to my grandmother, Frances, who was the best unrecognized chef in her time.

Johnny had a hard time convincing country musician Charlie
Daniels that a man's place could be in the kitchen, too.

TURKEY MEATBALLS IN SUNDAY SAUCE

1 pound ground turkey

About 1/2 cup fine plain bread crumbs

1/4 cup grated Parmesan cheese

3 tablespoons chopped flat-leaf parsley

2 eggs, beaten

1 tablespoon Johnny Ciao Opera Mix (see page 136 for substitutions)

1 tablespoon pine nuts

Olive oil for cooking

1 recipe Sunday Sauce (page 46)

*F*orget about beef and pork when making those famous Italian meatballs; use ground turkey instead. Try it with your own meatball recipe, or better yet, try mine.

*G*ently mix together turkey, bread crumbs, cheese, parsley, eggs, Johnny Ciao Opera Mix and pine nuts in a large bowl. If mixture is too moist, add more bread crumbs. Form 1/4 cupfuls of mixture into balls.

*H*eat about 1 inch olive oil in a skillet or deep-fryer. Add meatballs and fry until golden brown, but not thoroughly cooked, about 5 minutes. Drain on paper towels. Lower balls into simmering Sunday sauce and simmer 45 minutes. The meatballs will remain moist and juicy. Serve with sauce.

I've always looked forward to those hearty classic recipes like pot roast, beef stew and meatloaf. Here I've taken one of those oldies but goodies and remixed it, to make a much healthier version.

PSYCHEDELIC TURKEY MEATLOAF

1 pound ground turkey meat

3 whole eggs

About 1/3 cup fine plain bread crumbs

1/4 cup grated Italian cheese

1 bell pepper (use a mixture of colors), diced

1 small white onion, chopped

2 tablespoons chopped flat-leaf parsley

2 tablespoons pine nuts

1 tablespoon Johnny Ciao Opera Mix (see page 136 for substitutions)

1/2 tablespoon Johnny Ciao BarBQ Blues (see page 136 for substitutions)

Relish to serve

*P*reheat oven to 375F (190C). Mix together all ingredients except relish in a large bowl until well mixed. If mixture is too moist, then add more bread crumbs. Place mixture in a nonstick 9 × 5–inch loaf pan. Bake 45 minutes or until juices run clear when center of meatloaf is pierced with a knife. Let stand in pan 10 minutes. Slice and serve with relish.

SOULFUL SEAFOOD

SYMPHONIC SEAFOOD CIAO-DER

1/4 cup virgin olive oil

3 cloves garlic, minced

1 white onion, chopped

3 medium tomatoes, peeled and chopped

1 (15-oz.) can cannellini beans, drained

1 cup water

1 teaspoon dried mint leaves or 1 tablespoon chopped fresh mint

2 bay leaves

1/2 teaspoon crushed juniper berries

1 pound black mussels, cleaned

2 whole lobsters or Dungeness crabs, cleaned

1 pound large shrimp, shelled and deveined

1/2 pound white fish (halibut, hake, flounder)

Cooked pasta, rice or noodles to serve (optional)

Mint leaves to garnish

In a stockpot, heat oil over medium heat. Add garlic and onion. Cook 2 minutes, then add tomatoes, beans, water, mint, bay leaves and juniper berries. Cover and cook 12 to 15 minutes. Reduce heat to low. Add mussels and lobster or crab, cover and cook about 7 minutes or until mussels have opened and lobster or crabmeat is white. Remove mussels and lobster or crab, discarding any mussels that have not opened. Add shrimp and fish to pot, cover and cook over low heat 4 minutes. Remove meat from lobster or crab and cut into bite-size pieces. Remove mussels from the shells. Add lobster or crabmeat and mussels to mixture in stockpot. Simmer 5 minutes. Discard bay leaves. Pour over pasta, rice, or noodles, or eat as a soup. Garnish with mint leaves.

There is something special about the combination of fresh fish flavors coming together in a stew or soup. Creating good seafood chowder is like orchestrating a record. You start off with some rhythmic ingredients and work your way up to the string section. The more time spent nurturing and producing this next dish, the better it will sound. It's the kind of dish you create while having a kitchen party. Make some rhythm snax and trax, invite some friends and family over, and let it all hang out.

GRILLED HALIBUT WITH APPLE CIDER VINAIGRETTE

The marinade for this fish has lots of zing. You can adjust the amount of the chile to taste—*habañeros* are the world's hottest chiles.

2 tablespoons apple cider
   vinegar
1 clove garlic, minced
About 1 teaspoon minced
   habañero chile
2 tablespoons fresh orange
   juice

1 tablespoon fresh lime juice
1 teaspoon Johnny Ciao's
   Soulful Seafood (see page
   136 for substitutions)
1 1/2 pounds halibut fillets

Preheat broiler or oven to 375F (190C). Combine vinegar, garlic, chile, orange juice, lime juice and Johnny Ciao's Soulful Seafood in a baking pan just large enough to hold fish in a single layer. Add fish and turn to coat with juice mixture. Let stand 15 minutes. Broil fish 5 to 6 minutes or until just beginning to flake, or bake about 10 minutes. Serve hot.

GRILLED SWORDFISH WITH CITRUS SALSA

1 red grapefruit, peeled and
   sectioned

2 oranges, peeled and
   sectioned

2 limes, peeled and sectioned

1 lemon, peeled and sectioned

1 cup mixed bell pepper strips

1 medium red onion, finely
   diced

1 tablespoon chopped cilantro

1 tablespoon chopped mint

2 tablespoons tequila

1 tablespoon corn oil

4 (5-oz.) swordfish steaks

1 tablespoon Johnny Ciao's
   Soulful Seafood (see page
   136 for substitutions)

Citrus slices and mint leaves
   to garnish

To make the citrus salsa: Mix together the fruits, bell peppers, onion, cilantro, mint and tequila in a food processor or blender and process in pulses just to finely chop; do *not* overprocess into a liquid.

Preheat grill. Brush swordfish with corn oil and Johnny Ciao's Soulful Seafood. Arrange swordfish on grill and cook 3 minutes on each side or until swordfish just begins to flake. Spoon salsa over grilled fish. Garnish with citrus slices and mint leaves.

Whether you're indoors or out, grilling has become a year-round activity. Try this one in the dead of winter or on a rainy day on your indoor grill.

MAHI-MAHI BURGERS

MAKES 4 BURGERS

I love the idea of creating new and inventive ways to eat seafood. Here is my version of burgers from the sea. It'll blow you away. Low-fat, tasty and inventive.

1 pound mahi-mahi or ahi
  tuna, chopped
2 shallots, finely chopped
1 teaspoon prepared wasabi
2 teaspoons low-sodium soy
  sauce
1 tablespoon minced
  gingerroot

1 egg, beaten
1/4 cup dry bread crumbs
1 teaspoon Johnny Ciao's
  Rockin' Poultry (see page
  136 for substitutions)
1 tablespoon corn oil
Hot mustard to serve
French rolls to serve

*P*reheat grill or broiler. Mix fish, shallots, wasabi, soy sauce, gingerroot, egg, bread crumbs and Johnny Ciao's Rockin' Poultry together in a large bowl. Form mixture into 6 patties. Brush a grill rack or broiler pan with oil and arrange patties on grill or pan. Grill or broil 5 minutes, turning once, or until cooked through. Serve with mustard on French rolls.

CRAZED CATFISH

1/2 cup water

4 boneless catfish fillets

1 tablespoon minced
gingerroot

3 medium tomatoes, peeled
and chopped

5 whole green onions,
chopped

10 sprigs flat-leaf parsley or
sorrel, chopped

Salt and pepper (optional)

Steamed rice to serve

*P*our water into a skillet over medium-low heat. Add fish and arrange gingerroot, tomatoes, green onions and parsley on fish. Season with salt and pepper, if desired. Cover and cook 10 minutes or until fish just begins to flake. Serve with steamed rice.

*I*n the late 1970s, after leaving Florida and moving to Atlanta, Georgia, I began promoting jazz in venues like the historic Fox Theater. We booked artists like Stanley Turrentine, Ramsey Lewis, Eric Gale, Woody Shaw, and Jimmy Smith.

Since I promoted the concerts, I also wanted these jazz greats to sample my dishes, so I'd prepare lots of new things. Simple, yet inventive, here is a fish favorite enjoyed by some great legends of the jazz world.

HALIBUT IN TANGO SAUCE

This is a terrific dish for a special dinner party that combines the mellow tropical flavors of fresh mango with a ginger zip.

3 tablespoons peanut oil
1 large mango, peeled, pitted
    and chopped
1 large shallot, chopped
1 clove garlic, minced
1/2 teaspoon minced
    crystallized ginger
1 cup chicken broth

1 teaspoon Johnny Ciao's
    Jazzy Pepper (see page
    136 for substitutions)
4 (7-oz.) halibut steaks,
    1 inch thick
Fresh herb sprigs and lemon
    slices to garnish

Heat 2 tablespoons of the peanut oil in a skillet over medium heat. Add mango, shallot, garlic and ginger and cook about 5 minutes or until softened. Add chicken broth and cook until reduced by half. Remove from heat and cool mixture slightly. Spoon mixture into a blender or food processor and process until pureed. Add jazzy pepper; pulse to blend. Pour puree into a squeeze bottle.

Preheat grill or broiler. Brush fish with remaining peanut oil. Arrange fish on grill or broiler pan. Broil or grill about 5 minutes on each side or until fish just begins to flake. Arrange fish on plates. Garnish plate or fish with puree by squeezing puree into an interesting design. Top with herb sprigs and lemon slices.

PSYCHEDELIC JAWS

1 1/2 pounds thresher or other
shark
3 tablespoons light olive oil
1 tablespoon Johnny Ciao's
Soulful Seafood (see page
136 for substitutions)

1 each red, green and yellow
bell peppers
Fresh lime juice

Rinse shark and pat dry with paper towels. Place in a baking dish with 2 tablespoons of the olive oil and the Johnny Ciao's Soulful Seafood. Rub oil and seasoning gently into shark. Cover and refrigerate.

Preheat oven to 400F (205C). Rinse bell peppers, dry and lightly coat with remaining tablespoon olive oil. Arrange bell peppers on a baking sheet and bake 15 to 20 minutes or until blackened. Remove from oven and cool. Peel peppers and remove seeds. Cut peppers into strips, then process each one separately in a food processor or blender until smooth. Add lime juice to thin purees, if needed, making it easier to funnel the mixtures into their respective squeeze bottles.

Reduce oven temperature to 350F (175C). Bake fish 15 minutes or until it just begins to flake when tested with a fork. Arrange fish on plates. Decorate plates and/or cooked fish with psychedelic swirls of pureed bell peppers.

This dish is as colorful and easy to make as it is good to eat. It was a favorite on the daily menu at Michael Jackson's Neverland.

SANTA BARBARA SURFER SAUTÉ

For an appearance on "Live with Regis and Kathie Lee," I was asked to prepare a dish that I had cooked for one of my Hollywood clients. The Santa Barbara Surfer Sauté, using fish fresh from the waters off the Santa Barbara coast, was created for Gregory Peck and his wife, Veronique. This slowly simmered combo of fresh California ingredients was a real hit with the Pecks and with Regis, too. This recipe is featured in *Cooking with Regis & Kathie Lee.*

2 tablespoons virgin olive oil
1/2 large Maui onion or other
  sweet onion, chopped
1 clove garlic, minced
1 red bell pepper, chopped
2 Anaheim chiles, chopped
About 1 teaspoon minced
  habañero chile or to taste
1 large tomato, peeled and
  chopped

1 teaspoon capers, chopped
1 medium yellow squash,
  diced
1 1/2 pounds whitefish
6 to 8 fresh basil leaves
Cooked basmati, brown or
  wild rice to serve

Heat olive oil in a large skillet over medium heat. Add onion and garlic and sauté 1 minute. Add bell pepper, Anaheim chiles and habañero chile and cook 3 minutes. Reduce heat and add tomato and capers. Cover and cook 1 minute. Add squash and cook 5 minutes or until softened. Add fish and basil leaves. Cook 3 minutes or until fish just begins to flake.

Serve this dish over rice.

POACHED SAFFRON FISH FILLETS

2 tablespoons fresh lemon
    juice
1/4 cup white wine
1/4 cup water
1 teaspoon Johnny Ciao's
    Soulful Seafood (see page
    136 for substitutions)
1 teaspoon Johnny Ciao's
    Country Herbs (see page
    136 for substitutions)

1 bay leaf
1/2 teaspoon saffron threads
2 shallots, finely chopped
2 large salmon fillets
6 to 8 flat-leaf parsley sprigs,
    chopped

Place all ingredients except fish and parsley in a large skillet. Cover and cook over medium heat 5 minutes, bringing mixture to a boil. Reduce heat and add fish, skin side up, and parsley to the skillet. Cook, covered, over low heat about 5 minutes, or until skin easily flakes off with a fork. Discard bay leaf. Transfer fish to a plate or platter and spoon on cooking juices.

During my stay at Neverland Valley, I was given the opportunity to cook for several people I like to call "The Reclusives." One of those people was the legendary Marlon Brando. When it was announced that he was on his way up from the front gate, which is approximately two miles away from the main house, I got pretty nervous. I felt like Vito Corleone was on his way up.

In response to my inquiry about what he would like to eat, Mr. Brando requested poached fish and a cabbage salad with vinegar and lemon juice. I concocted this recipe to counter what I thought might be pretty boring fare for one of the world's most famous people. It's easy, light and healthy, but the wonderful combination of herbs and spices gives it terrific taste appeal.

During the Fancy Food Show in New York City one year, I met a group of Spaniards who introduced me to a stash of some really fine saffron from La Mancha, in the Spanish highlands. I always thought that Italian and Iranian saffron was good stuff, so we debated for hours on which country had the finest threads.

The following week, I threw a dinner party for a group of real estate tycoons, so I figured that I'd sample the saffron from La Mancha. This lobster in a delicate saffron broth was the result.

2 large whole Maine lobsters
    (2 to 3 lbs. each)
1/4 cup virgin olive oil
3 cloves garlic, minced
3 shallots, chopped
1 1/2 cups tomato puree
1 teaspoon Johnny Ciao's
    Soulful Seafood (see page
    136 for substitutions)

1/2 cup cannellini beans,
    pureed
1/2 teaspoon saffron threads
1 cup cooked rice

Kill each lobster by placing on a flat surface, stomach side down. Insert the tip of a sharp knife into the lobster at the place where the tail and body join, severing the spinal cord. Cut lobsters in half lengthwise. Remove the stomach sac near the eyes and the intestinal vein that runs down the tail. Rinse lobsters and set aside.

Heat olive oil in a large pot over medium heat. Add garlic and shallots and sauté until softened, about 5 minutes. Add tomato puree and Johnny Ciao's Soulful Seafood, cover and cook 5 minutes over medium heat. Reduce heat and add lobsters to pot. Cover and simmer 10 minutes or until lobster meat is white. Remove lobsters and let cool. Add bean puree and saffron to mixture in pot. Increase heat under pot to medium-low and cook 10 minutes. Meanwhile, remove all meat from lobster shells and chop into bite-size pieces, reserving small claws for garnish. Add lobster pieces to pot and simmer 3 minutes. Serve over cooked rice. Use small claws as garnish.

THREE-MINUTE SCALLOPS

2 tablespoons virgin olive oil

2 cloves garlic, minced

1/4 cup dry white wine

1 teaspoon dried parsley

Juice of 1/2 lemon

1 pound fresh bay scallops, rinsed and patted dry

*H*eat olive oil in a medium skillet over medium heat. Add garlic and sauté 1 minute. Add wine, parsley and lemon juice. Cover and cook 1 minute. Add scallops and cook 1 minute or until scallops turn from translucent to opaque.

*H*ere's one of those in-the-pinch, quick shellfish dishes that's simply delicious. You've got to try these. A tasty treat!

LOUISIANA SHRIMP CREOLE

Some like it hot, and why not. This dish seems to be a favorite of many of my rock 'n' roll and blues musician friends. Put on your favorite sounds and chow down to this Creole treat.

1/4 cup vegetable oil

3 cloves garlic, minced

1 medium white onion, chopped

1 red bell pepper, chopped

2 celery stalks, finely chopped

1 cup tomato puree

1/2 cup water or wine

3 bay leaves

1 tablespoon Johnny Ciao's Soulful Seafood (see page 136 for substitutions)

1 tablespoon Tabasco sauce or to taste

1 pound large shrimp, shelled, deveined and cut into large chunks

Cooked Arborio or basmati rice to serve

Heat vegetable oil in a large saucepan over medium heat. Add garlic, onion, bell pepper and celery and sauté 4 minutes or until softened. Reduce heat to low and add tomato puree, water or wine, bay leaves, Johnny Ciao's Soulful Seafood and Tabasco sauce. Cover and simmer 20 minutes, stirring occasionally. Add shrimp and cook 2 minutes or until shrimp turn pink. Discard bay leaves. Serve over rice.

SHIITAKE PRAWNS WITH GRILLED LEEKS

2 tablespoons peanut oil

1/2 teaspoon minced
gingerroot

1 cup chopped leeks (white
part only)

1/4 cup vegetable stock or broth

1/4 cup soy sauce

1 teaspoon hot chile paste

1 teaspoon Johnny Ciao's
Soulful Seafood (see page
136 for substitutions)

1/2 pound shiitake
mushrooms, chopped

1 (4-oz.) can water chestnuts,
drained, rinsed and sliced

1 pound large prawns,
shelled and deveined

Cooked Chinese noodles or
brown rice to serve

A quick stir-fry dish that's easy to pre-pare and tastes outrageous! You can make it in your wok or in a large skillet.

Heat oil in a wok over high heat. Add gingerroot and leeks and stir-fry 3 minutes. Add stock or broth, soy sauce, chile paste and Johnny Ciao's Soulful Seafood. Reduce heat and cook until liquid is reduced by half and leeks are soft, about 10 minutes. Add mushrooms and water chest-nuts and stir-fry 3 minutes over high heat. Add prawns and stir-fry until pink, about 2 minutes. Serve over Chinese noo-dles or brown rice.

RED SNAPPER BURGER

1 pound fresh red snapper
    fillet, finely chopped

3 egg whites

2 tablespoons chopped
    green onion

1 tablespoon white
    Worcestershire sauce

1/2 cup dry bread crumbs

1 tablespoon Johnny Ciao's
    Soulful Seafood (see page
    136 for substitutions)

1 tablespoon vegetable oil

Horseradish Marinade (page
    115)

1 loaf French or Italian bread,
    sliced

4 fresh spinach leaves

With so many people eliminating beef from their diets, I've had to come up with alternative burger dishes, and my Red Snapper Burger is one great choice. From Michael Jackson to Henry Mancini to Ray Stevens, many of my clients have enjoyed this recipe, and I'm sure you will too. A beautiful orchestration of protein and flavor.

Preheat grill or broiler. Mix together fish, egg whites, green onion, Worcestershire sauce, bread crumbs and Johnny Ciao's Soulful Seafood in a large bowl. Form fish mixture into 4 patties.

Brush a grill rack or broiler pan with oil and arrange patties on grill or pan. Grill or broil 1 1/2 to 2 minutes on each side or until cooked through. Place a dab of Horseradish Marinade on each burger. Serve on French bread, topped off with a spinach leaf.

VOLCANIC SQUID

1/4 cup virgin olive oil

2 cloves garlic, minced

1 pound calamari (squid), cleaned

4 green olives, pitted and chopped

1 teaspoon capers, chopped

1/4 cup white wine

1 tablespoon Johnny Ciao's Opera Mix (see page 136 for substitutions)

1 (12-oz.) can tomato puree

1/2 cup sliced white button mushrooms

Heat olive oil in a deep skillet over high heat. Add garlic and squid and sauté 1 minute. Add green olives, capers and white wine and cook 2 minutes. Reduce heat to medium and add Johnny Ciao's Opera Mix, tomato puree and mushrooms. Cover and cook on low heat 20 minutes or until squid is tender, stirring occasionally.

A fiery and tasty way to prepare those squiggly creatures from the deep.

**Willie Nelson at his annual picnic in
Atlanta had a taste of
Johnny's impromptu Texas Prawn Stew.**

TEXAS PRAWN STEW

2 tablespoons virgin olive oil

3 cloves garlic, minced

1 jalapeño chile, minced

2 medium carrots, sliced

1 green bell pepper, chopped

1 medium zucchini, sliced

3 Roma tomatoes, peeled and
    chopped

1 cup sliced button mushrooms

1/2 cup water

2 (19-oz.) cans kidney or
    cannellini beans, drained

12 flat-leaf parsley sprigs,
    chopped

2 teaspoons Johnny Ciao's
    BarBQ Blues (see page
    136 for substitutions)

1 pound large shrimp or
    prawns, shelled
    and deveined

2 cups basmati rice, cooked

Heat olive oil in a large skillet over medium heat. Add garlic, chile, carrots and bell pepper and sauté 5 minutes or until soft. Add zucchini, tomatoes, mushrooms, water and beans. Cover and cook over low to medium heat 10 minutes, stirring occasionally. Add parsley, Johnny Ciao's BarBQ Blues and shrimp. Simmer, covered, 3 minutes or until shrimp turn pink. Pour over rice in bowls and serve.

While backstage at a Willie Nelson Picnic one year, I was coerced into creating some munchies for Willie, Waylon Jennings, Hank Williams, Jr., Merle Haggard, Linda Ronstadt and their friends. From the on-site caterers dishing out the usual country fare, I hustled up whatever ingredients I could: there was plenty of Texas basmati rice, some canned beans, assorted vegetables and giant fresh Gulf shrimp. Here's what I put together in one of those old giant iron skillets.

Meaty Orchestrations

B & B VENISON

4 medium venison medallions

2 tablespoons B & B Liqueur

2 tablespoons virgin olive oil

2 cloves garlic, minced

1 shallot, minced

1 cup low-sodium beef broth

2 tablespoons nonfat sour cream

1 tablespoon Johnny Ciao's Country Herbs (see page 136 for substitutions)

Marinate venison in B & B in a shallow bowl 1 hour. Heat a heavy skillet over high heat. Drain venison, reserving liqueur. Add venison to skillet and cook 3 minutes on each side, then remove from skillet. Add olive oil to skillet. Add garlic and shallot and sauté 1 minute over medium heat. Add venison and reserved liqueur and heat until hot. Carefully ignite and flame meat, allowing fire to burn out. Remove venison and add beef broth to skillet. Boil 5 minutes or until liquid is reduced by 75 percent. Reduce heat to low and stir in sour cream and Johnny Ciao's Country Herbs. Cook 1 minute. Return venison to skillet and heat through, then serve.

Since I was twelve years old, I've lived in the country. Even to this day I have a home in upstate New York, and when the fall comes rolling around, there are more deer in my backyard than birds. Personally I am not a hunter, although many of my friends are, so they bring me all kinds of wild game to cook up. This happens to be one of my venison dishes, which you can easily substitute with pheasant, wild boar or even wild turkey.

Food writer and critic Narcy David joined Johnny at the
Asparagus Festival in Stockton, CA.

BEEFY ASPARAGUS FAJITAS

1 pound beef loin steak, cubed

2 tablespoons olive oil

2 cloves garlic, minced

1 teaspoon minced gingerroot

1/2 jalapeño chile, minced

1 large tomato, peeled and
  chopped

1/2 cup chopped asparagus
  spears

1 teaspoon Johnny Ciao's
  Rockin' Poultry (see page
  136 for substitutions)

8 whole-wheat tortillas,
  warmed

1/4 cup shredded Monterey
  Jack cheese

Preheat oven to 400F (205C). Brown beef in a heavy skillet over medium heat, turning to brown all sides, then remove from skillet. Heat olive oil in same skillet. Add garlic, gingerroot and chile and sauté 1 minute. Add tomato, asparagus and Johnny Ciao's Rockin' Poultry. Cover and cook over medium heat 4 minutes. Drain off any liquid. Spoon beef mixture onto tortillas and sprinkle with cheese. Roll tortillas, carefully tucking in ends, to enclose beef mixture. Arrange rolled tortillas on a baking sheet. Bake 5 minutes to melt cheese.

One year I was asked to perform at the Annual Asparagus Festival in Stockton, California. In the middle of asparagus farms, this big three-day event featured live entertainment, country activities and, of course, lots of asparagus treats. These fajitas captured the spirit of the event and the essence of Californian-Mexican cuisine.

CITRUS SCALOPPINI

For a live demonstration/performance/audition set up in a restaurant on Melrose Avenue in Hollywood, I had to prepare a meal in less time than it takes to microwave a "TV dinner." I recreated a frozen citrus veal scaloppini that was cheaper and fresher than its frozen food counterpart and contained no chemicals. Under five minutes for under five dollars, this one should be a busy-day hit.

1 egg
1 cup whole-wheat flour
1/2 cup rolled oats
1 tablespoon grated citrus peel
2 tablespoons light olive oil
1 pound veal, turkey or
    chicken cutlets

1 tablespoon butter
1/2 cup fresh orange juice
1 teaspoon juniper berries,
    crushed
Citrus slices and mint sprigs
    to garnish

Beat egg in a shallow bowl. Combine flour, oats and citrus peel in another shallow bowl. Dip cutlets in egg, then into flour mixture, coating both sides. Heat olive oil in a large skillet over medium heat. Add coated cutlets and cook 1 minute on each side. Remove cutlets and place on paper towels to drain.

Meanwhile, melt butter in another skillet over medium heat. Add orange juice and juniper berries, and boil until liquid is reduced by half. Add cutlets to reduced mixture. Cook over low heat about 30 seconds on each side to heat through. Transfer cutlets and sauce to plates. Garnish with citrus slices and mint sprigs.

HERBED CALF LIVER WITH CARAMELIZED LEEKS

1/2 cup all-purpose flour

1/2 cup fine plain bread crumbs

2 teaspoons Johnny Ciao's
   BarBQ Blues (see page 136
   for substitutions)

1 pound calf liver

4 tablespoons virgin olive oil

1 tablespoon butter

2 leeks, chopped

1/2 cup vegetable stock or
   broth

1 tablespoon sherry vinegar

2 tablespoons light
   brown sugar

Combine flour, bread crumbs and Johnny Ciao's BarBQ Blues in a shallow bowl. Coat each piece of liver with flour mixture. Heat 3 tablespoons of the olive oil in a large skillet over medium heat. Add liver and cook until browned on both sides, turning. Remove from skillet.

In another skillet, heat butter and remaining tablespoon olive oil over medium heat until butter melts. Add leeks and vegetable stock or broth. Cook, covered, 10 minutes or until leeks soften. Uncover and boil until liquid is reduced by half. Reduce heat, add vinegar and brown sugar and stir until caramelized, about 5 minutes. Add liver to leeks and cook 3 minutes on each side. Transfer liver to plates and top with leeks and sauce.

As a kid, I despised the smell and taste of any kind of liver, but now it's one of my favorite animal parts to eat. I guarantee that after you create this simple dish, it'll become a favorite of yours as well.

If you like the flavor of lamb, then you must try this rich and delicious lamb shank recipe. You'll even want to eat the bone, because it tastes so good.

BRAISED LAMB SHANKS IN PORCINI CREAM SAUCE

1 cup boiling water

2 ounces dried porcini
mushrooms

1 cup all-purpose flour

2 teaspoons Johnny Ciao's
Country Herbs (see page
136 for substitutions)

4 whole lamb shanks

1/4 cup virgin olive oil

4 cloves garlic, minced

2 onions, chopped

2 cups dry white wine

1 cup chicken broth

1/4 cup coarse-grain mustard

1/2 cup whipping cream

8 flat-leaf parsley sprigs, finely
chopped

Cooked egg noodles to serve

Pour boiling water over mushrooms and let stand 15 minutes. Drain mushrooms, reserving liquid, and chop.

Preheat oven to 350F (175C). Mix together flour and Johnny Ciao's Country Herbs in a shallow bowl. Coat lamb with flour mixture and shake off excess. Heat olive oil in a Dutch oven over medium heat. Add lamb shanks and bake until browned on all sides, about 30 minutes.

Remove lamb shanks and place on paper towels to drain. Add garlic and onions to drippings in Dutch oven and cook over medium heat 5 minutes. Stir in porcini mushrooms, mushroom soaking liquid, wine, broth and mustard, and bring to a boil. Reduce heat and return shanks to pan. Simmer, covered, 90 minutes or until lamb is tender and falling off bone.

Remove lamb and set aside. Stir in cream and parsley and cook, stirring, over medium heat until liquid is reduced by half. Reduce heat to low and return lamb to pan, turning to coat with sauce. Cover and cook about 5 minutes to heat through. Serve lamb and sauce over egg noodles.

SOY PORK CHOPS

6 tablespoons soy sauce

2 tablespoons honey

3 tablespoons peanut oil

2 tablespoons red wine
   vinegar

1 tablespoon Johnny Ciao's
   BarBQ Blues (see page
   136 for substitutions)

1 teaspoon powdered ginger

3 cloves garlic, minced

6 (1-inch-thick) pork chops

I've always been a pork lover. Its tender white meat has a flavor like no other, and its possibilities in the kitchen are endless.

Mix all ingredients except pork chops in a shallow bowl. Add pork chops and turn to coat with mixture. Cover and refrigerate several hours or overnight, turning occasionally.

Preheat broiler or grill. Remove pork chops from the marinade, reserving marinade. Place pork chops on grill or in a broiler pan. Grill or broil, not too close to the heat, 15 minutes. Baste with reserved marinade. Turn and cook 10 to 15 minutes or until no longer pink in center.

CALIFORNIA-STYLE SPEDINI

*T*his is quite a delicate and exotic dish, yet surprisingly simple to prepare. Once again, I've taken one of those oldie but goodie Italian dishes, and turned it around.

1 pound veal, turkey or chicken
   cutlets

2 eggs, beaten

1/4 cup fine plain bread crumbs

2 tablespoons grated
   Parmesan cheese

8 whole basil leaves, chopped

1 cup spinach leaves, finely
   chopped

1 tablespoon pine nuts,
   chopped

2 tablespoons goat cheese

1 tablespoon virgin olive oil

1/2 cup tomato puree

*P*reheat oven to 375F (190C). Place cutlets between two sheets of waxed paper and pound until extra thin. Mix together eggs, bread crumbs, cheese, basil, spinach and pine nuts in a medium bowl. Mixture should be sticky and pasty. Lightly spread each cutlet with egg mixture. Place a dab of goat cheese on each cutlet, then carefully roll up, placing a wooden pick through each one to hold it firmly in place. Place rolled cutlets in a baking dish, brush with olive oil, then cover with tomato puree. Bake 20 to 30 minutes or until medium browned. Remove picks and carefully slice each one into 1-inch-thick slices. Serve over pasta.

SPICY PORK CUTLETS

1 tablespoon virgin olive oil

Juice of 1/2 lemon

1/4 teaspoon minced dried
  habañero chile

1 teaspoon minced
  crystallized ginger

1/2 teaspoon ground coriander

1 tablespoon dried cilantro or
  parsley

1 pound thinly sliced pork
  cutlets

*P*reheat oven to 350F (175C). Grease a baking sheet. Mix together all ingredients except cutlets in a shallow bowl. Coat cutlets with spicy mixture and arrange in a single layer on baking sheet. Bake 15 to 20 minutes, depending on thickness, until cooked through. Serve with Asparagus Opera Patties (page 101), if desired.

*E*very now and then it's good for your blood to eat something just a little spicy. I came up with this East Indian/Mexican–flavored spicy pork dish one afternoon while experimenting with *habañero* chiles. These are one of the hottest chiles on the planet, so be very cautious how much you use. Do not touch your eyes or face after chopping this chile. This dish may be eaten as prepared, or it can be cut up into smaller pieces and placed in tortillas, to make an Indian burrito.

```
NEVERLAND VALLEY MENU

MAY 5, 1989

_____


ACT I

Turkey Bracciole rolled and stuffed with
herbs, cheese, and pine nuts


ACT II

Banana Squash Leek Soup


ACT III

Chicory and Pistachio Nut Salad


ACT IV

Grilled Mahi-Mahi with a red bell pepper sauce
                or
Veal Filet Tenderloin with sun dried tomatoes
in a raspberry vinaigrette
                or
Grilled Porterhouse/New York Strip Steak
                or
Chicken Parmigiana with Spinach Raviolli


ACT V

Banana Cream Pie
        or
Cinammon Bananas with Cream
        or
Chocolate Mousse
```

**One of the many menus created for Michael Jackson and
his Neverland guests. Mr. and Mrs. Gregory Peck chose
the Veal Filet Tenderloin.**

VEAL TENDERLOIN WITH SUN-DRIED TOMATOES IN RASPBERRY VINAIGRETTE

2 pounds whole veal
   tenderloin
4 tablespoons olive oil
1/4 teaspoon salt
2 tablespoons Johnny Ciao's
   Country Herbs (see page
   136 for substitutions)

1/2 cup raspberry vinegar
12 sun-dried tomatoes soaked
   in sherry

Preheat oven to 400F (205C). Rub veal with some of the olive oil, salt and Johnny Ciao's Country Herbs. Place in a roasting pan. Roast 45 minutes for rare or to desired doneness. Thinly slice across grain. Whisk together remaining olive oil and raspberry vinegar in a small bowl. Slice tomatoes into thin strips and place on each piece of meat. Then drizzle the oil/vinegar mixture over meat and tomatoes. Serve at room temperature.

For a dinner for ten to be hosted by one of my non-celebrity Hollywood clients, this veal dish was ideal because it can be served at room temperature—he had a habit of postponing the beginning of his dinners sometimes by hours. But there were no complaints from the guests, including Lionel Richie, Scott Baio, and Princess Stephanie.

Country singer Brenda Lee on the set of
Cooking with Country Music Stars.

STEAK PIZZAOLA

2 tablespoons virgin olive oil

2 cloves garlic, minced

1 (12-oz.) can tomato puree

2 tablespoons grated
    Parmesan cheese

1 teaspoon Johnny Ciao's
    Opera Mix (see page 136
    for substitutions)

4 flat-leaf parsley sprigs,
    chopped

2 (1-inch-thick) beef
    porterhouse or shell steaks

1/2 pound spaghetti, cooked

*H*eat olive oil in a large skillet over medium-low heat. Add garlic and sauté 1 minute. Add tomato puree and simmer 10 minutes. Add cheese, Johnny Ciao's Opera Mix, parsley and steaks, and simmer 6 to 8 minutes on each side, turning, or until cooked to desired doneness. Serve steak and sauce over spaghetti.

*H*ow about a tasty and out-of-the-ordinary steak dinner? This steak should be eaten with spaghetti, because the sauce is out of this world and should not go to waste.

JOHNNY'S VEAL STEW

*C*reating good stew depends on how much time you want to spend with it while it's cooking. Sure, you can just toss everything in a slow cooker or pressure cooker, but I like to put special vibes into each ingredient along the way. I'll play my harmonica or timbales or just meditate, and believe me, it works. Just like anything else in life, the more you pay attention, the better the outcome.

1/4 cup virgin olive oil

1 1/2 pounds veal cubes

1 teaspoon minced gingerroot

1 clove garlic, minced

1 small onion, chopped

1 Anaheim chile, chopped

2 large tomatoes, peeled and chopped

2 carrots, sliced

4 small red potatoes, diced

1/2 pound oyster mushrooms, thinly sliced

1 bay leaf

1 teaspoon crushed juniper berries

1/2 cup water

8 fresh mint leaves, chopped

Cooked noodles or rice to serve

*H*eat olive oil in a Dutch oven over medium heat. Add veal cubes and cook, turning, until browned on all sides. Remove veal from oil with a slotted spoon and place in a bowl. Add gingerroot, garlic, onion and chile to drippings in pan and cook over medium heat 3 minutes. Add tomatoes, carrots, potatoes, mushrooms, bay leaf, juniper berries and water. Cover and cook on low heat 30 minutes. Add browned veal and mint leaves and cook 20 minutes or until veal and vegetables are very tender. Discard bay leaf. Serve over noodles or rice.

Variation

To create a thicker sauce, drain off cooking liquid, add a little flour mixed with cold water and cook in a small saucepan, stirring, until thickened. Stir into stew ingredients.

Veggie Vocals

TRI-COLORED STUFFED BELLS

8 mixed yellow, green and red
  bell peppers

1/4 cup virgin olive oil

3 cloves garlic, minced

1 1/2 teaspoons capers,
  chopped

1 tablespoon chopped Gaeta
  olives

1 teaspoon Johnny Ciao's
  Opera Mix (see page 136
  for substitutions)

8 to 10 flat-leaf parsley sprigs,
  chopped

1/2 cup water

2 bunches escarole, chopped

1/2 cup fine plain bread
  crumbs

3 tablespoons grated
  Parmesan or Romano
  cheese

1 egg, beaten

This is a wonderful meal on its own or a great side dish to accompany any meal. It may be prepared in advance, and tastes incredible even a day or two after. You can also freeze it for later use.

Preheat oven to 400F (205C). Rub each bell pepper with oil. Place in a large baking dish and bake 20 minutes or until blistered, then remove and cool. Drain off any excess liquid. Peel bell peppers and remove stems, cores and seeds; set peppers aside.

In a large pot, heat remaining oil over medium-low heat. Add garlic, capers and olives and sauté 2 minutes. Add Johnny Ciao's Opera Mix, parsley and water. Cover and cook 2 minutes, then add escarole. Cook, covered, until escarole is soft and tender, about 10 minutes. Remove from heat and drain off liquid. Set aside to cool.

Preheat oven to 350F (175C). Place escarole in a large bowl. Stir in bread crumbs, cheese and egg. Spoon escarole mixture into bell peppers. Arrange stuffed peppers in a baking dish and bake 20 minutes or until filling is very hot. Serve warm or at room temperature.

CARROT YAM SMASH

*W*hat wonderful sounds you'll capture when you mix these two top veggie vocalists and create a smash hit. Kids will love this one.

6 carrots, cut into large chunks

2 yams or sweet potatoes, peeled and cut into large chunks

1 teaspoon ground nutmeg

1 teaspoon Johnny Ciao's Country Herbs (see page 136 for substitutions)

2 tablespoons chopped flat-leaf fresh parsley

*C*ook yams and carrots separately in boiling water until soft. Drain carrots and sweet potatoes and place in a large bowl. Add remaining ingredients and mash. Or process in a food processor until pureed for a finer texture. Serve hot as a side dish.

FIDDLER'S FAVAS

2 pounds fresh fava beans

1 tablespoon virgin olive oil

1 clove garlic, minced

1/2 cup water

1 tablespoon Johnny Ciao's Country Herbs or Opera Mix (see page 136 for substitutions)

1/4 pound goat cheese, cut into 4 or 5 pieces

*R*emove fava beans from pods, peel individual beans and separate into halves. Heat olive oil in a large skillet over medium heat. Add garlic and sauté 1 minute. Add water, beans and Johnny Ciao's Country Herbs or Opera Mix. Reduce heat to low, cover and cook 15 minutes or until beans are tender.

*P*reheat oven to 400F (205C). Drain beans and place in a medium baking dish. Top with goat cheese. Bake 5 minutes or until goat cheese is very soft. Serve with chicken or beef dishes.

*F*ava beans are seasonal, and most people don't know what to do with them. They're full of vitamins and other nutrients—and this is a great way to get your protein, calcium, vitamins A and C . . .

CARAMELIZED ONIONS

*T*hese sweet-tasting onions are fabulous with baked chicken, mashed potatoes, liver, steak, pork chops and lots more. They are simple to prepare and will impress everyone who tastes them.

2 tablespoons butter
2 tablespoons virgin olive oil
1 teaspoon crushed juniper berries
4 to 6 medium Vidalia onions or other sweet onions, thinly sliced

3 tablespoons light brown sugar
2 tablespoons cognac

*M*elt butter with olive oil in a large skillet over medium heat. Add juniper berries and onions, cover, and cook about 8 minutes, stirring occasionally, or until onions are soft. Add a little water if onions are too dry. Add brown sugar and cook, stirring, about 5 minutes or until caramelized. Add cognac, heat until hot and carefully ignite. Let burn until flames burn out. Pour onions over an entree, or eat as a side dish.

ASPARAGUS OPERA PATTIES

1 pound asparagus, trimmed

2 eggs, beaten

1/3 cup fine plain bread
   crumbs

1/4 cup grated Parmesan
   cheese

1 teaspoon dried parsley

2 tablespoons virgin olive oil

Tomato Basil Mayonnaise
   (page 113) to serve

Cook asparagus in a pot of boiling water until soft, about 10 minutes. Remove and cut into small pieces or mash. Combine asparagus and all remaining ingredients except olive oil and mayonnaise in a medium bowl and mix well. Form into 16 patties.

Heat oil in a large skillet over medium heat. Arrange patties in hot oil and cook 1 to 2 minutes on each side or until browned. Serve warm or at room temperature with Tomato Basil Mayonnaise.

Opera has always played a significant role in my life. It was everywhere while I was growing up. One day several friends popped in for lunch at my Woody Trail house in the Hollywood Hills. It turned out that these L.A. hipsters, who were fanatic opera fans, were going to see "The Three Tenors," Pavarotti, Domingo and Carreras at Dodger Stadium that evening, and they asked me if I'd like to go. Bummer, I couldn't make it. But I was in the kitchen partying all day, whipping up all kinds of goodies. I proceeded to pack up a batch of this recipe for them to munch on while taking in the concert. Great for ballgames as well, these patties are safe to transport and taste great hours after they're cooked.

SCARY CARROTS

*W*ow, what can I say? It's only carrots, yet this dish tastes so good, it's scary!

1 pound organic carrots
1 cup water
1 tablespoon butter
1/2 teaspoon freshly grated gingerroot

1 teaspoon fresh lemon juice
1 teaspoon chopped fresh tarragon

*P*eel and trim carrots. Cut crosswise into 1-inch-thick slices, and steam in a medium saucepan over boiling water until tender, about 10 minutes. Spoon carrots into a serving dish. In a separate saucepan, melt butter over medium heat. Add gingerroot, lemon juice and tarragon. Cook 1 minute, then pour over carrots. Serve immediately.

GINGER-SPICED CAULIFLOWER

1 (4-inch) piece gingerroot,
　　chopped

3 cloves garlic

1 teaspoon Johnny Ciao's
　　Soulful Seafood (see page
　　136 for substitutions)

1 tablespoon ground coriander

1/4 cup virgin olive oil

2 cups vegetable stock
　　or broth

2 medium heads cauliflower,
　　cut into 1-inch chunks

Juice of 2 lemons

1 red or green bell pepper,
　　finely chopped

3 tablespoons chopped
　　cilantro

This is a spicy, Indian-flavored vegetarian dish that also goes great alongside lamb, chicken or beef. For a vegetarian meal, serve with lentils or basmati rice.

Place gingerroot, garlic, Johnny Ciao's Soulful Seafood, coriander, olive oil and 1/2 cup of the vegetable stock or broth in a blender and puree until smooth. Pour mixture into a large skillet. Add cauliflower to pureed mixture and cook over high heat 1 minute. Add remaining 1 1/2 cups stock and bring to a boil, stirring constantly. Reduce heat to medium and cook until cauliflower is crisp-tender, 5 to 7 minutes. Add lemon juice, bell pepper and cilantro and cook 5 minutes. Serve hot.

SPANISH RICE

This rice dish is almost a whole meal unto itself, but it can jazz up the simplest of fish and chicken dishes.

1 cup long-grain white rice
3 tablespoons vegetable oil
1 pound lean ground beef
1/2 large onion, chopped
1 clove garlic, minced
1/2 green bell pepper, chopped

3 cups stewed tomatoes
1 teaspoon Johnny Ciao's Opera Mix (see page 136 for substitutions)
2 teaspoons chile powder

Rinse rice, drain and allow to dry thoroughly. Heat oil in a heavy skillet over medium heat. Add rice and cook 5 minutes. Add beef, onion, garlic and bell pepper. Cook until beef is browned, stirring to break up beef. Add undrained tomatoes, Johnny Ciao's Opera Mix and chile powder. Reduce heat to low, cover and cook 30 minutes, stirring occasionally, or until rice is tender and liquid is absorbed. Add water if needed to finish cooking rice. Let stand 5 minutes before serving.

VEGGIE RISOTTO

1/4 cup virgin olive oil

2 tablespoons unsalted butter

2 cloves garlic, minced

1 small onion, chopped

1 medium red or green bell
   pepper, chopped

1 cup arborio rice

2 medium carrots, thinly sliced

1 medium yellow squash,
   finely chopped

1 cup chopped broccoli
   flowerets

4 medium roma tomatoes,
   peeled and chopped

1/2 teaspoon saffron threads

1 tablespoon Johnny Ciao's
   Country Herbs or Opera
   Mix (see page 136 for
   substitutions)

5 cups vegetable broth

10 sprigs flat-leaf parsley,
   chopped

*R*isotto is a time-consuming dish but well worth the effort. It's another one of those in-the-kitchen party dishes. Make some appetizers to munch before you start this one. A creamy, rich and very healthy treat.

*I*n a deep skillet or pot, heat oil and butter over medium heat. Add garlic, onion and bell pepper and sauté 3 minutes. Add rice and cook, stirring constantly, to coat with oil mixture. Add remaining ingredients except broth and parsley.

*B*ring broth to a boil in a separate saucepan. Slowly add the hot broth to the rice mixture, stirring constantly, about 1/2 cup at a time. Reduce heat to low. Cook, stirring, about 45 minutes or until broth is absorbed and rice is tender. Stir in parsley. Can be served alone or as a side dish.

Drummin' Dips, Marinades and Dressings

OLIVE TOMATO DIP

3 large tomatoes

8 Greek ripe olives, pitted

1 teaspoon sugar

1/3 cup plain low-fat yogurt

1 teaspoon Johnny Ciao's
   Opera Mix (see page 136
   for substitutions)

5 fresh basil leaves, chopped

Submerge whole tomatoes in boiling hot water for 30 seconds. Remove with a slotted spoon and place in iced water to cool. Peel tomatoes and cut into large pieces. Combine tomatoes, olives, sugar, yogurt and Johnny Ciao's Opera Mix in a food processor or blender and process until smooth. Stir in chopped basil and serve.

GINGER LIME DIP

1/4 teaspoon salt

1/4 teaspoon dry mustard

1/2 teaspoon ground ginger

2 teaspoons grated lemon peel

1 teaspoon dried mint leaves

1/2 cup safflower oil

1 egg yolk

2 tablespoons fresh lime juice

*I*n a small bowl, mix salt, dry mustard, ginger, lemon peel, mint and oil until well blended. Whisk in egg yolk and lemon juice. Just before serving, whisk until well blended. This tangy and delectable treat is great with fried snax.

# ORANGE SALSA

2 cups orange sections
1/2 cup finely chopped red
    onion
1/2 cup finely chopped jicama
2 tablespoons finely chopped
    red bell pepper

2 tablespoons fresh lime juice
1 tablespoon jalapeño chile,
    minced
1 teaspoon garlic powder

Combine all ingredients in a medium bowl. Cover and refrigerate until chilled. It goes with just about everything from chicken to fish to pork.

PISTACHIO NUT DRESSING

1 1/2 tablespoons hot water

1 teaspoon saffron threads

1 teaspoon honey

1/2 cup safflower oil

2 teaspoons white wine
   vinegar

1/2 teaspoon Johnny Ciao's
   Jazzy Pepper (see page
   136 for substitutions)

1 1/2 tablespoons pistachio
   nuts, finely chopped

*M*ix hot water, saffron and honey in a small bowl, then refrigerate 15 minutes. In a separate bowl, mix oil, vinegar and Johnny Ciao's Jazzy Pepper and add to refrigerated mixture. Stir in pistachios and serve.

TOMATO BASIL MAYONNAISE

3 medium tomatoes, peeled,
  seeded and chopped

2/3 cup low-fat mayonnaise

1 teaspoon minced garlic

1 tablespoon chopped fresh
  chives

1 tablespoon plain low-fat
  yogurt

1 teaspoon sugar

1 tablespoon Johnny Ciao's
  Opera Mix (see page 136
  for substitutions)

1 tablespoon chopped fresh
  basil

*C*ombine all ingredients in a food processor or blender and process until pureed. Cover and refrigerate until chilled. Serve with grilled chicken or fish.

JUNIPER BERRY DRESSING

1 tablespoon juniper berries,
   well crushed

1/3 cup walnut oil

1/4 teaspoon ground cinnamon

1 tablespoon fresh lemon juice

1 tablespoon minced walnuts

*F*inely chop juniper berries. In a small bowl, mix together juniper berries, oil, cinnamon and lemon juice. Add walnuts and serve over mixed greens or fruit.

HORSERADISH MARINADE

2 tablespoons horseradish

1 1/2 tablespoons plain nonfat
   yogurt

1 teaspoon Johnny Ciao's
   BarBQ Blues (see page 136
   for substitutions)

1 tablespoon chopped fresh
   thyme leaves

1 teaspoon Johnny Ciao's Jazzy
   Pepper (see page 136 for
   substitutions)

1/2 teaspoon white wine
   vinegar

1 teaspoon safflower oil

Mix all ingredients together in the bowl to be used for marinating the meat. Use as a marinade for steaks, pork chops, chicken breasts and other cuts of meat.

AVOCADO DRESSING

1 avocado, peeled and pitted

1 tablespoon fresh lemon juice

1/2 cup mayonnaise

1/4 cup safflower oil

1 garlic clove

1/4 teaspoon Tabasco sauce

1/2 teaspoon Johnny Ciao's
Soulful Seafood (see page
136 for substitutions)

*C*ut avocado into chunks. Combine all ingredients in a food processor or blender and process until smooth. Serve as a dip or salad dressing.

CALIFORNIA DUDE SALSA

2 cups peeled and chopped
   fresh tomatoes

1 celery stalk, chopped

1 medium onion, chopped

1 jalapeño chile, chopped

1 tablespoon virgin olive oil

1 teaspoon Johnny Ciao's
   Rockin' Poultry (see page
   136 for substitutions)

1 tablespoon sugar

1 tablespoon chopped fresh
   cilantro

1 teaspoon red wine vinegar

Combine all ingredients in a food processor or blender and process until coarsely blended. Serve with tortilla chips or as an accompaniment to fish dishes.

JOHNNY'S GUAC AND ROLL

2 avocados, peeled and pitted

1 tablespoon safflower oil

2 whole green onions, chopped

1 tablespoon fresh lemon juice

1/2 teaspoon oregano

Dash of cumin

*C*ut avocado into chunks. Combine all ingredients in a medium bowl. Mash with a fork into a coarse consistency. Serve with tortilla chips or as garnish for other meals.

JOHNNY'S SWEET AND SPICY SAUCE

1 (32-oz.) can low-sodium V8
    vegetable juice
1 cup water
1/4 cup all-natural red currant
    jelly
1/4 cup arrowroot mixed with
    1/2 cup water

1 teaspoon ground cumin
1/2 teaspoon ground sage
Vegtaballs (page 15),
    Zucchini Flowers (page
    13) or chicken and fish
    dishes to serve as dippers

In a medium pot, mix vegetable juice, water and jelly. Bring to a boil over medium heat. Remove from heat and stir in the arrowroot mixture. Cook, stirring constantly over medium heat until thickened and clear. Stir in cumin and sage. Serve hot.

VEGETABLE SALSA

1 tablespoon fresh lemon juice

2 tablespoons virgin olive oil

1/2 red bell pepper, diced

1/2 green bell pepper, diced

1 cucumber, peeled, seeded
   and diced

1 medium red onion, diced

1 green onion, chopped

1 teaspoon Johnny Ciao's
   BarBQ Blues (see page
   136 for substitutions)

Whisk lemon juice and olive oil together in a medium bowl. Add remaining ingredients and toss to combine. Serve with tortillas or as an accompaniment to other dishes.

FINAL NOTES

BANANA BLUES

2 tablespoons butter

1/2 cup packed light brown sugar

1 shot (2 tablespoons) milk

1 shot (2 tablespoons) banana liqueur

2 whole bananas, cut into quarters

1 dash of ground cinnamon

1 shot (2 tablespoons) cognac

4 large scoops vanilla ice cream

Melt butter in a large nonstick saucepan over medium heat. Stir in brown sugar until moistened. Add milk and banana liqueur and cook, stirring, until smooth. Add bananas and cinnamon and cook 1 minute, then carefully turn bananas. Add cognac and flame 1 minute, then pour banana mixture over vanilla ice cream.

On one of my television appearances, I worked with a harmonica legend named Little Sammy Davis. Sammy has performed with many of the blues greats, including Earl Hooker, Little Walter and Muddy Waters, and while he is close to seventy years old, he continues to blow some mean harp. He loved bananas, so I created a banana dessert on the spot while Sammy played his harmonicas. That's the day the banana blues were born.

SWINGING POACHED PEARS IN CHOCOLATE SAUCE

Some desserts are decadent, and some are even more decadent. This is one of the few that I prepare that falls into the *more* decadent category. I think the indulgence may be worth it.

2 (750-ml.) bottles (6 cups) white Burgundy wine

1 cup granulated sugar

5 whole cloves

3 cinnamon sticks

6 large fresh pears, cored, peeled and halved

1 cup whipping cream

4 squares semisweet chocolate

2 1/2 cups powdered sugar

1/3 cup butter

2/3 cup espresso or strong coffee

Vanilla ice cream to serve (optional)

Bring the wine, granulated sugar, cloves and cinnamon sticks to a boil in a large saucepan over high heat. Reduce heat and add pears. Simmer, covered, until just tender; do *not* overcook. Set aside until cool.

Combine cream, chocolate, powdered sugar, butter and coffee in the top part of a double boiler. Place over hot, not boiling water, and cook 30 minutes, stirring occasionally.

Spoon chocolate sauce into 6 stemmed glass dessert dishes. Drain the pears and place 2 pear halves in each dish. Or serve pears over vanilla ice cream and top with the chocolate sauce.

CHUCK BERRIES SOLO DESSERT TOPPING

2 tablespoons butter

1 teaspoon vanilla extract

1 cup cranberry juice

2 tablespoons sugar

1/4 cup fresh cranberries

1/4 cup dried figs or dates, finely chopped

1/4 cup walnuts, chopped

1 teaspoon ground cinnamon

Ice cream to serve

Melt butter in a heavy saucepan over medium heat. Add vanilla, juice, sugar and cranberries and cook over high heat 5 to 7 minutes or until cranberries pop open. Reduce heat, add figs or dates, walnuts and cinnamon and simmer 3 minutes. Pour over ice cream and enjoy.

If you like those sweet and hard-driving sounds of the guitar, then you're going to love this ice cream jamming session.

FIGS WITH PEPPERCORN SAUCE AND BASIL

*T*his recipe can be made with fresh or dried figs although the dried variety is much easier to come by. This spicy dessert with its suprisingly seasoned sauce will keep you coming back for more.

1/2 cup white peppercorns, crushed

3 cups water

1 bunch fresh basil, chopped

1 cup white wine

2 cups sugar

2 cups dried figs, cut in half

Ice cream or pound cake to serve (optional)

Basil and whole white peppercorns to decorate

*P*lace peppercorns, water, basil and wine in a heavy saucepan and bring to a boil over high heat. Boil 10 minutes and strain mixture through a fine strainer. Return liquid to saucepan, add sugar and cook, stirring occasionally, 5 minutes over high heat or until mixture is thick and syruplike. Add figs and cook over medium heat 10 minutes, or until figs are tender. Serve figs in plates or over ice cream or pound cake. Decorate with basil leaves and whole peppercorns.

BROILED FIGS

12 to 16 fresh figs

1 tablespoon sugar

2 tablespoons fruit preserves

1 tablespoon rum

2 teaspoons fresh lime juice

1/2 teaspoon grated lime peel

4 fresh mint leaves, finely chopped

*P*reheat broiler. Rinse figs and place in a shallow casserole dish. Sprinkle sugar over figs. Broil 4 to 5 minutes or until a sugar glaze forms on each one. In a small bowl, mix together preserves, rum, lime juice, lime peel and mint. Pour mixture over hot figs and serve.

*H*ere's a simple, yet elegant dessert using my favorite fruit, the fig. My grandfather grew figs in his backyard, and I'll never forget scrambling up the tree, during visits to his house, so I could get my share of them before my cousins did.

BAKED PEARS WITH CRÈME FRAÎCHE

I like to keep my desserts simple and fruity.

1/4 cup dark rum

6 pears

1 cup packed light brown sugar

3 tablespoons unsalted butter

2 teaspoons grated nutmeg

1 cup crème fraîche,
sour cream or ice cream

*P*reheat oven to 375F (190C). Pour the rum into a shallow baking dish. Cut pears in half and remove cores. Place the pears, brown sugar and butter in baking dish. Bake 15 minutes. Sprinkle with nutmeg and baste with pan juices. Bake 10 minutes or until pears are just tender. Top with creme fraîche, sour cream or ice cream.

GINGER BERRY SHORTCAKE

1 cup fresh strawberries,
  hulled and halved

1 tablespoon cream sherry

2 tablespoons raspberry
  spread

1/8 teaspoon ground ginger

1 dash of ground cinnamon

4 ready-to-serve shortcakes

Vanilla frozen yogurt

*J*ust another one of my fruity overdubs. Outrageous and simple.

*C*ombine strawberries, sherry, spread, ginger and cinnamon in a small bowl. Place a large scoop of yogurt on each shortcake and top with strawberry mixture.

NUTTY SNOWBALLS

This is a great holiday dessert that your kids can help with.

1/4 cup almonds, finely diced

1/4 cup hazelnuts, finely diced

1/2 cup powdered sugar, sifted

3 egg whites

Additional powdered sugar for coating

Preheat oven to 350F (175C). Line a baking sheet with waxed paper. In a small bowl, mix nuts together. Add sugar and slowly stir in 1 egg white to form a paste.

With your hands, form nut paste into 24 small round balls. In a small bowl, whisk remaining 2 egg whites lightly until frothy. Dip balls into egg whites, then roll in powdered sugar to coat. Place balls in paper baking cases or muffin tin liners, then place on baking sheet. Bake 12 to 15 minutes or until golden brown on top and firm. Remove from baking sheet and cool. Sift powdered sugar over tops.

GLOSSARY

Anaheim chiles are cultivated in Mexico, Central America and the American Southwest. These chiles are mild and sweet tasting.

Arborio rice is a short-grain rice with a high-starch content, which makes it perfect for risotto.

Arrowroot is a starchlike substance used as a thickener in soups and sauces. Use in same amounts as cornstarch.

Basil is an herb native to tropical Asia. In India, it was considered a protector against evil. In Italy, it was long considered a love charm. Basil has a minty, clovelike aroma and can be found in a number of varieties, including sweet basil, purple or oval basil and lemon basil.

Basmati rice is a long-grain rice with a nutlike flavor and aroma.

Belgian endive grows from the root of one kind of chicory plant that is kept in total darkness. It is a compact head of long, thin leaves of pale yellow and white, with green tips. It is crunchy, with a pleasantly bitter flavor that complements milder greens or stands well on its own.

Bouillon is a seasoned broth or stock produced by cooking meats and fish in liquid. It is used as a base in many dishes.

Cannellini beans are white kidney beans. They are available either dried or canned.

Canola oil is a bland-tasting oil produced from grape seed. It is high in monounsaturated fats and contains Omega-3 fatty acids.

Capers are unopened flower buds of the caper bush, usually pickled in vinegar or bottled in salt. A great seasoning, its peppery flavor adds a nice spark of magic to pasta sauces, cold meats and fish.

Celery seed is the strong-flavored seed from wild celery or lovage.

Chile powder is pure ground dried hot chiles as apposed to *chili powder*, which is a blend of seasonings used for making chili con carne.

Chili paste is a salty, spicy paste of beans, chiles, flour, and sometimes garlic, used as a seasoning in many Chinese and Southeast Asian dishes.

Cilantro is a leafy green herb also known as coriander or Chinese parsley.

Coriander is the seed of the cilantro or coriander plant and is used in Indian, Mexican, North African and Chinese dishes.

Crème fraîche is a thickened cream that can be purchased or made at home by adding 2 tablespoons yogurt, buttermilk or sour cream to 1 cup heavy cream, which is then covered and left at room temperature for several hours or until thickened. It is often used in desserts and sauces.

Crystallized ginger is gingerroot that has been cooked in a sugar syrup.

Cumin is an aromatic seed used to flavor Indian, Oriental and Latin American dishes. Also used in powdered or ground form.

Dill is a flavorful herb used in soups and stews, and on chicken, fish and vegetables. Both the feathery green leaves and the seed are used.

Escarole is another form of endive, similar in flavor to Belgian endive or curly leaf endive but with a milder flavor. It is slightly bitter in taste, but cooked down with some garlic and olive oil or simply blanched, it has a fabulous flavor.

Farfalle is a butterfly or bow-tie shaped pasta.

Fava beans are tan, flat beans that are removed from their pods and peeled before cooking. They are similar in shape to lima beans.

Fennel seed is the seed from an herb plant with tall green stalks, feathery leaves and a licoricelike flavor. The Greeks and Romans believed it gave strength, courage, long life and good eyesight.

Gaeta olives are small to medium-size black olives with a smooth-textured skin, slightly salty in taste.

Ginger is available fresh as gingerroot or dried and ground into a powder. Each form has its own distinctive flavor. Also see **Crystallized ginger**.

Goat cheese (chèvre) is a tart white cheese made from goat's milk. Montrachet is one type that is readily available.

Gorgonzola cheese, a creamy Italian blue cheese named after a town near Milan, has a slightly pungent aroma. It is good with fruit or used in cooking.

Habañero chile is one of the hottest chiles—use with caution in cooking. It is available fresh or dried.

Horseradish is available as grated horseradish in bottles, as the fresh root and dried as a powder. It has a strong pungent flavor.

Jalapeño chile is a small, medium-heat chile, usually green or red.

Jicama is a large, juicy, crunchy and nutritious root from Mexico and the American Southwest. It is peeled, sliced and mostly eaten raw in salads.

Juniper berries are pungent dried blue-black berries that are used to flavor many meat dishes and provide gin with its distinctive bouquet and taste.

Leeks, a relative of the onion, are cultivated for their pale green leaves and white stalks. Leeks have a strong odor that becomes more subtle when cooked. Clean leeks well because there are large amounts of sand within the layers. It is easiest to do this by slitting the leeks almost through from top to bottom, then rinsing under cold water. They are much easier to digest than onions and scallions.

Mango is a fleshy tropical fruit with a sweet and tart flavor and a large flat seed. Mangoes are in season May through September.

Mint, one of the most familiar tastes, flavors toothpastes, chewing gums, teas and many foods. There are over forty varieties of mint. Spearmint and peppermint are the most common ones used in cooking. Fresh mint has more flavor than dried mint and is preferred for cooking.

Nutmeg, a tropical evergreen tree, gives us both the spices nutmeg and mace, the latter of which is a lacy membrane covering the nutmeg seed. Freshly ground or grated nutmeg has a flavor superior to that of commercially ground.

Oregano is an aromatic herb that is used in many Italian dishes. It is related to marjoram, but is considered a bit sharper in flavor.

Oyster mushrooms are small fan-shaped mushrooms with a robust flavor. They are available both wild and cultivated.

Paprika is a red powder made by grinding the dried pods of sweet red bell peppers. It can range from mild to hot.

Parmesan cheese comprises a group of hard, dry Italian cheeses that are aged up to four years. It is usually grated, which is best done just before using. Related cheese types include Reggiano, Lodigiano, Lombardo, Emiliano, Venato and Brescianno.

Pine nuts, also known as pignoli or piñons, are blanched pine cone seeds with an aromatic and rustic flavor. They are used on salads and in stuffings for meat dishes as well as for baked goods.

Porcini mushrooms, the king of mushrooms, possess a rich and exquisite meaty flavor. They are used in soups and pastas.

Portobello mushrooms, a very large dark-brown mushroom, are the mature version of the crimino. They are often grilled.

Prosciutto, a salt-cured, air-dried ham from Italy, is often cut into paper-thin slices and eaten with fruit.

Radicchio is a small red chicory with white leaves that can be mixed with other salad greens or grilled with olive oil. It has a tangy, yet bitter flavor, and its beautiful ruby red color adds a further dimension to salads.

Rosemary, a pungent and refreshing herb with needlelike leaves, is the symbol of remembrance. Used quite often with chicken dishes, it has a piney aroma and a spicy, minty flavor.

Saffron, the dried stamens of a crocus, is the most expensive spice in the world at over $150.00 per ounce. It originated in Spain, Italy and the Middle East. It is used sparingly to give color and flavor to dishes.

Savory, an herb similar to thyme, has a spicy, peppery flavor.

Scallions (green onions), bulbless onions with hollow green tops and a white base, have a mild onion flavor.

Shallots, a relative of both the onion and garlic, have the flavor of both.

Shiitake mushrooms, Oriental mushrooms whose name means "oak fungus," are available fresh or dried. They are great stir-fried or grilled.

Sweet onions are medium to large onions with a sweeter flavor than most onions. Examples include the Maui onion from Hawaii and the Vidalia onion from Georgia. Sweet onions are delicious raw or cooked.

Tarragon is an herb with long, slender, deep-green leaves that grow along the stems. It has a mild aniselike aroma and flavor, with a slight tartness. It is known as an exhilarating herb.

Tellicherry pepper, from India, is one of the best black peppers.

Thyme has a pleasant aroma and flavor, somewhat like a blend of sage and clove.

Turmeric, a root related to ginger, is widely available as a powder. A common ingredient in curry powder, turmeric adds a yellow color to foods.

Wasabi, available in paste and powdered forms, is from the root of an Asian plant and is often called "Japanese horseradish." Wasabi has a strong pungent flavor. It is wonderful with sashimi, sushi or other fish dishes.

Water chestnuts, available canned and fresh, grow under water. Peel fresh ones before using. They add a sweet crunchiness to stir-fried and other dishes.

White peppercorns are berries of the pepper vine that are allowed to ripen, then the skins are removed and the berries are dried. White peppercorns have a flavor milder than that of black peppercorns.

Zest, or grated citrus peel, contains aromatic oils that impart flavor to foods.

JOHNNY CIAO'S SEASONINGS

*J*ohnny Ciao's seasonings are available by mail order.

The Johnny Ciao six-pack of seasonings includes:

Jazzy Pepper   Rockin' Poultry
Soulful Seafood   Opera Mix
BarBQ Blues   Country Herbs

Send check or money order in the amount of $18.00
Plus $3.00 (shipping/handling) to:

JOHNNY CIAO SEASONINGS
P.O. BOX 652
GREENWOOD LAKE, N.Y. 10925

Allow 4–6 weeks for delivery.

Johnny's Web site address in http://campus. net

All of the herbs and spices are naturally blended and bottled by Vanns Spices in Baltimore, Maryland, and are of the highest quality available.

The following is a list of the seasonings as well as substitutions that can be made for each blend. Throughout this book, I use my seasonings in most recipes, as they cut down preparation time.

If you prefer to use your own spices and herbs, the recipes will taste just as good using the most basic and simplest herbs and spices that you probably already have. Similar flavors may be obtained by using the following herbs and spices within a particular recipe.

Substitution List

Name of Seasoning	Ingredient Substitutions (Use equal parts for all.)
BarBQ Blues	chile powder, onion powder, paprika, Worcestershire sauce, garlic
Country Herbs	basil, thyme, rosemary, savory, fennel seed
Soulful Seafood	onion powder, garlic, cumin, turmeric
Rockin' Poultry	ground ginger, herbed pepper, lemon, dill, celery seed, onion powder
Jazzy Pepper	tellicherry and green peppercorns, shallots, garlic, brandy
Opera Mix	oregano, basil, minced onion, garlic powder, garlic pepper

INDEX

A

Aglio e Olio con Verdura, 35
Asparagus
   Asparagus Opera Patties, 101
   Beefy Asparagus Fajitas, 83
Avocado
   Avocado Dressing, 116
   Johnny's Guac and Roll, 118

B

B & B Venison, 81
Baked Oriental Chicken, 52
Baked Pears with Créme Fraîche, 128
Banana Blues, 123
Beans
   Black Bean Soup, 20
   Escarole and Bean Soup, 22
   Fiddler's Favas, 99
   Pasta Fagiola, 36
   Psychedelic Bean Salad, 29
   Sting Bean Salad, 31
Beef
   Beefy Asparagus Fajitas, 83
   Steak Pizzaola, 93
Black Bean Soup, 20
Bluesy Burrito, 11

Braised Lamb Shanks in Porcini
   Cream Sauce, 86
Broccoli
   Vegtaballs, 14
Burritos
   Bluesy Burrito, 11

C

California Dude Salsa, 117
California-Style Spedini, 88
Caramelized Onions, 100
Carrots
   Carrot Ginger Vichyssoise, 21
   Carrot Yam Smash, 98
   Scary Carrots, 102
Catfish
   Crazed Catfish, 65
Cauliflower
   Ginger-Spiced Cauliflower, 103
Chicken
   Baked Oriental Chicken, 52
   California-Style Spedini, 88
   Citrus Scaloppini, 84
   Electrifying Chicken Breasts, 50
   Honey-Glazed Chicken Strips, 8
   Oatmeal Chicken Breasts, 51
   Old-Fashioned Hen Soup, 19

Chicken (*cont.*)
    Peppermint Chicken Wings, 9
    Radicchio Chicken Tacos, 53
    Shroom and Shallot Chicken Pasta,
        45
    Sicilian Hens in Machine Gun Broth,
        55
Chuck Berries Solo Dessert Topping, 125
Ciao's Creamy Light Turkey, 49
Citrus Scaloppini, 84
Cold Pasta Primavera, 39
Cornish hens
    Sicilian Hens in Machine Gun Broth,
        55
Corny Shrimp, 5
Crazed Catfish, 65

D
Desserts
    Baked Pears with Crème Fraîche,
        128
    Banana Blues, 123
    Broiled Figs, 127
    Chuck Berries Solo Dessert Topping,
        125
    Figs with Peppercorn Sauce and
        Basil, 126
    Ginger Berry Shortcake, 129
    Nutty Snowballs, 130
    Swinging Poached Pears in
        Chocolate Sauce, 124
Dilled Mussels, 6
Dips
    Ginger Lime Dip, 110
    Johnny's Guac and Roll, 118
    Olive Tomato Dip, 109
Dixieland Tomato Bisque, 25

Dressings
    Avocado Dressing, 116
    Juniper Berry Dressing, 114
    Pistachio Nut Dressing, 112

E
Electrifying Chicken Breasts, 50
Escarole
    Escarole and Bean Soup, 22

F
Farfalle Porcini, 38
Fiddler's Favas, 99
Figs
    Broiled Figs, 127
    Figs with Peppercorn Sauce and
        Basil, 126
Fish. See Seafood/fish
Fruit Boats, 7

G
Ginger Berry Shortcake, 129
Ginger Lime Dip, 110
Ginger-Spiced Cauliflower, 103
Great Balls of Fire, 3
Grilled Halibut with Apple Cider
    Vinaigrette, 62
Grilled Swordfish with Citrus Salsa, 63

H
Halibut
    Grilled Halibut with Apple Cider
        Vinaigrette, 62
    Halibut in Tango Sauce, 66

Herbed Calf Liver with Caramelized
    Leeks, 85
Honey-Glazed Chicken Strips, 8
Horseradish Marinade, 115

J

Johnny's Sweet and Spicy Sauce, 119
Johnny's Veal Stew, 94
Juniper Berry Dressing, 114

L

Lamb
    Braised Lamb Shanks in Porcini
        Cream Sauce, 86
Liver
    Herbed Calf Liver with Caramelized
        Leeks, 85
Lobster
    Saffron Lobster, 70
Louisiana Shrimp Creole, 72

M

Mahi-Mahi Burgers, 64
Marinade
    Horseradish Marinade, 115
Mayonnaise, Tomato Basil
        Mayonnaise, 113
Meatballs
    Turkey Meatballs in Sunday Sauce, 58
Meatloaf
    Psychedelic Turkey Meatloaf, 58
Meat. See specific types of meat.
Mom's Zucchini Soup, 26
Mushrooms
    Farfalle Porcini, 38

Shroom and Shallot Chicken Pasta, 45
Mussels
    Dilled Mussels, 6
    Potato Mussel Salad, 30

N

New Age Pasta Fagiola, 37
Nutty Snowballs, 130

O

Oatmeal Chicken Breasts, 51
Old-Fashioned Hen Soup, 19
Olive Tomato Dip, 109
Onions
    Caramelized Onions, 100
Orange Salsa, 111

P

Pasta
    Aglio e Olio con Verdura, 35
    Cold Pasta Primavera, 39
    Farfalle Porcini, 38
    New Age Pasta Fagiola, 37
    Pasta Alla Gratte, 42
    Pasta Creamavera, 39
    Pink Shellfish Pasta, 41
    Salmon Basilico, 44
    Shroom and Shallot Chicken Pasta, 45
    Spaghetti Putanesca, 43
Pasta sauce
    Sunday Sauce, 46
Pearberry Soup, 24
Pears
    Baked Pears with Crème Fraîche,
        128

Pears (*cont.*)
   Swinging Poached Pears in
      Chocolate Sauce, 124
Peppermint Chicken Wings, 9
Peppers
   Tri-Colored Stuffed Bells, 97
Pink Shellfish Pasta, 41
Pistachio Nut Dressing, 112
Poached Saffron Fish Fillets, 69
Pop Salad, 27
Pork
   Soy Pork Chops, 87
   Spicy Pork Cutlets, 89
Potatoes
   Potato Mussel Salad, 30
Prawns
   Shiitake Prawns with Grilled Leeks, 73
   Texas Prawn Stew, 76
Psychedelic Bean Salad, 29
Psychedelic Jaws, 67
Psychedelic Turkey Meatloaf, 58
Pumpkin Leek Soup, 23

R
Radicchio Chicken Tacos, 53
Red Snapper Burger, 74
Rice
   Rice Balls, 10
   Spanish Rice, 104
   Veggie Risotto, 105
Rice Balls, 10
Risotto
   Veggie Risotto, 105

S
Saffron Lobster, 70

Salads
   Fruit Boats, 7
   Pop Salad, 27
   Potato Mussel Salad, 30
   Psychedelic Bean Salad, 28
   Sting Bean Salad, 31
Salmon
   Poached Saffron Fish Fillets, 69
   Salmon Basilico, 44
Salsa
   California Dude Salsa, 117
   Orange Salsa, 111
   Vegetable Salsa, 120
Santa Barbara Surfer Sauté, 68
Sauces
   Johnny's Sweet and Spicy Sauce, 119
   Sunday Sauce, 46
Sausage
   Great Balls of Fire, 3
Scallops
   Three-Minute Scallops, 71
Scary Carrots, 102
Seafood/fish
   Corny Shrimp, 5
   Crazed Catfish, 65
   Dilled Mussels, 6
   Grilled Halibut with Apple Cider
      Vinaigrette, 62
   Grilled Swordfish with Citrus Salsa,
      63
   Halibut in Tango Sauce, 66
   Louisiana Shrimp Creole, 72
   Mahi-Mahi Burgers, 64
   Pink Shellfish Pasta, 41
   Poached Saffron Fish Fillets, 69
   Potato Mussel Salad, 30
   Psychedelic Jaws, 67
   Red Snapper Burger, 74

Saffron Lobster, 70
Santa Barbara Surfer Sauté, 68
Shiitake Prawns with Grilled Leeks,
    73
Symphonic Seafood Ciao-Der, 61
Texas Prawn Stew, 76
Three-Minute Scallops, 71
Volcanic Squid, 75
Seasonings
    address for ordering, 135
    substitution list, 136
Shark
    Psychedelic Jaws, 67
Shiitake Prawns with Grilled Leeks, 73
Sicilian Hens in Machine Gun Broth,
    55
Shortcake
    Ginger Berry Shortcake, 129
Shrimp
    Corny Shrimp, 5
    Louisiana Shrimp Creole, 72
    Shroom and Shallot Chicken Pasta, 45
Snacks
    Bluesy Burrito, 11
    Corny Shrimp, 4
    Dilled Mussels, 6
    Fruit Boats, 7
    Great Balls of Fire, 3
    Honey-Glazed Chicken Strips, 8
    Peppermint Chicken Wings, 9
    Rice Balls, 10
    Vegtaballs, 14
    Zucchini Flowers with Ginger Lime
        Dip, 13
    Zucchini Sushi Drum Rolls, 12
Soups
    Black Bean Soup, 20
    Carrot Ginger Vichyssoise, 21

Dixieland Tomato Bisque, 25
    Escarole and Bean Soup, 22
    Mom's Zucchini Soup, 26
    Old-Fashioned Hen Soup, 19
    Pearberry Soup, 24
    Pumpkin Leek Soup, 23
Soy Pork Chops, 87
Spaghetti Putanesca, 43
Spanish Rice, 104
Spicy Pork Cutlets, 89
Squid
    Volcanic Squid, 75
Steak Pizzaola, 93
Stew
    Johnny's Veal Stew, 94
    Texas Prawn Stew, 77
Stuffed Turkey Rotolo, 54
Sunday Sauce, 46
Sweet potatoes
    Carrot Yam Smash, 98
Swinging Poached Pears in Chocolate
    Sauce, 124
Swordfish
    Grilled Swordfish with Citrus Salsa,
        63

T
Texas Prawn Stew, 77
Three-Minute Scallops, 71
Tomato Basil Mayonnaise, 113
Tomatoes
    Dixieland Tomato Bisque, 25
    Sunday Sauce, 46
Toppings
    Chuck Berries Solo Dessert Topping,
        125
Tri-Colored Stuffed Bells, 97

Turkey
    California-Style Spedini, 88
    Ciao's Creamy Light Turkey, 49
    Citrus Scaloppini, 84
    Psychedelic Turkey Meatloaf, 58
    Stuffed Turkey Rotolo, 54
    Turkey Meatballs in Sunday Sauce,
        57

V

Veal
    California-Style Spedini, 88
    Citrus Scaloppini, 84
    Johnny's Veal Stew, 94
    Veal Tenderloin with Sun-Dried
        Tomatoes in Raspberry
        Vinaigrette, 91
Vegetable Salsa, 120

Veggie Risotto, 105
Vegtaballs, 15
Venison
    B & B Venison, 81
    Beefy Asparagus Fajitas, 82
Volcanic Squid, 75

W

Whitefish
    Santa Barbara Surfer Sauté, 68

Z

Zucchini
    Mom's Zucchini Soup, 26
    Zucchini Flowers with Ginger Lime
        Dip, 13
    Zucchini Sushi Drum Rolls, 12

Johnny Ciao, popularly known as the "Culinary Rocker," has cooked with and for some of the biggest names in the entertainment, sports and political worlds. His outrageous presentations of food and music have landed him dozens of guest spots on national and local television and radio shows, and generated feature articles in newspapers and magazines.

As a spokesperson for a number of food-related products, his blend of culinary expertise and entertainment has been showcased at department stores and trade shows around the country.

A native of New York, he divides his time among Atlanta, where he recently opened the Celebrity Rock Cafe, Los Angeles and New York.